Bingo The Winner

Autum Augusta

Order this book online at www.trafford.com
or email orders@trafford.com

Most Trafford titles are also available at major online book retailers.

Printed in the United States of America.

ISBN: 978-1-4669-6531-7 (sc)
ISBN: 978-1-4669-6533-1 (hc)
ISBN: 978-1-4669-6532-4 (e)

Library of Congress Control Number: 2012920250

Trafford rev. 11/05/2012

 www.trafford.com

North America & international
toll-free: 1 888 232 4444 (USA & Canada)
phone: 250 383 6864 ✦ fax: 812 355 4082

CONTENTS

Sambo the watch dog.

Bingo the Winner

CHAPTER I

Sambo and Lucky

Sambo looked toward the large, old, farm house. He looked up and down the country road that passed the farm. It was Sambo's duty to protect the farm from intruders and bark when something, or someone, came too close to the farm. There was not a strange animal or person in sight. Sambo shook his head when a large bee flew by his ear. He stretched out his large, coyote-looking body and took another nap.

Suddenly, Sambo's ears stood up. He heard a truck coming down the road. He jumped to his feet and began to bark. Sambo's tail started wagging when he recognized Joe's red, four-wheel-drive pickup truck. He greeted Joe as Joe crawled down from the large vehicle.

Joe patted Sambo on the head and walked toward the house.

Sambo followed Joe up the back steps to the kitchen door.

Joe patted Sambo's furry head just before he went into the house and closed the door.

Sambo laid down on the back step and began watching the road again. He barked when a small calf poked its head through one of the wooden fences located beyond the back yard. "Protecting this place is hard work," Sambo thought as he laid his head down on his front paws.

Sambo heard Joe opening the door. He moved out of the way and followed Joe out to the pickup truck. Sambo waited for another love pat on the head.

"When Betty and I are married, Sambo, we're going to move to town. You won't have to work so hard to protect our house in town," Joe said. He patted Sambo again and crawled back into the pickup truck.

Sambo watched Joe's vehicle back away from the house and drive out of sight on the dusty, country road. He lay down next to the road to watch over his territory again.

It was getting dark when Sambo smelled a terrible odor. Sambo's nose started burning. He rubbed his nose with his paw. The odor was sickening. "It's that awful black and white cat that makes that awful smell," Sambo told himself. He ran to the chicken house north of the farmhouse. Sambo barked and growled several times before the skunk came out of the chicken house. Sambo barked and growled louder.

The skunk ignored Sambo. He slowly waddled into the weeds at the edge of the field. The skunk was full of fresh eggs and he did not want to walk fast.

Sambo watched the skunk go through the weeds until he was out of sight. He remembered the time he had gotten too close to the skunk and the skunk sprayed him with the awful smelling stuff. Sambo eyes and nose had hurt and he had gotten sick at his stomach. Sambo was glad the skunk did not want to make trouble this time.

Sambo was rubbing his nose when he saw the weeds move again. He barked at the large Bull snake that was slithering along the side of the chicken house. The snake was also hungry for eggs, but this time he wiggled back into the weeds. Maybe the chicken house smelled too terrible or he did not like Sambo's barking.

Sambo checked the cattle pens. Everything looked all right. He walked back across the yard and drank some cool water from the pan next to the house.

It was soon dark. Sambo barked when he saw car lights coming down the country road toward the house. He barked until the car passed by the farm and Sambo could no longer see the lights. "I protected the farm that time," Sambo said to himself. He lay down to nap again. Sambo moved a little closer to the house when he heard coyotes howling. He did not know that he was half coyote, and that his daddy was a coyote.

Sambo was still watching the farm when Joe came home from his date that night.

The next night Betty came back with Joe for supper. Joe fixed some steak and potatoes. He gave Sambo the steak bones to eat.

Sambo liked Betty. She talked softly and patted his head. Every time Betty came to the farm, Sambo ran to meet her and put one paw on her lap. After Betty patted him on the head, Sambo would be so embarrassed that he would run and hide.

Joe and Betty were married in April. Joe moved his clothes to Betty's house in town, then he came back to the farm for Sambo.

Sambo had never been inside a car before. He was afraid when Joe lifted him up and pushed him onto the front seat of the pickup truck. His body was stiff and shaking as Joe drove the twelve miles into town.

Joe pulled Sambo from the truck and carried him into the house. "I'm glad to see you, Sambo," Betty said. She fed him some people-food leftovers for supper.

Joe put a leash on Sambo's collar and took him for a walk after supper. Sambo had to learn where the new property lines were.

Sambo slept in the house that night beside Joe and Betty's bed. The next day, after Betty went to work, Joe showed Sambo their property line again. "Stay close to the house and off the busy street," Joe told Sambo.

Sambo watched Joe's red pickup truck leave town on its way back to the farm. He laid down on the front porch to rest. He quickly jumped to his feet and started barking at a car coming down the street. Sambo barked at another car and another car.

Sambo had never lived in town. When he saw all the cars going by, he felt confused. He did not know which ones to bark at. Sambo finally gave up trying to bark at all the cars. He lay down again to rest on the front porch of Betty's house. "It's going to be very hard to protect Joe and Betty in this place," Sambo said to himself.

Sambo was almost asleep when he heard a thumping noise.

He looked up and saw two large dogs running right at him. Sambo was frightened. He ran and jumped on top of Joe and Betty's new car.

The two dogs barked and growled. They barked and growled until they were too tired to bark anymore. The two dogs finally went back home to the house next door. The dogs crawled back into their own yard through a tunnel they had dug under the back yard fence.

"Oh, no, those mean dogs can crawl out of their yard and chase me any time they want to," Sambo thought.

Sambo was afraid to jump off the car. He took a nap on the top of the car. Sambo was still asleep when Joe and Betty came home from work. He heard them yelling at him.

"Get off our new car, Sambo!" Joe shouted. "You'll scratch it and make marks on it!" he yelled.

Sambo jumped off the car. He flattened his body and crawled under the car. Sambo was afraid that the two mean dogs might come over again.

The next day the two dogs chased Sambo again. He barely made it to the car in time. Sambo jumped back up on the car. This time Sambo watched the house so he could jump down when he saw Joe or Betty standing at the door.

Betty brought Sambo some chicken bones left over from dinner. "Sambo, I know you are still jumping on our new car," Betty said. "It has scratch marks on it!" Betty exclaimed. Betty was sad.

Sambo was sad. He did not like to make Betty unhappy, but he did not know any other way to get away from the two mean dogs.

Joe was sitting in his chair, reading his newspaper.

One evening Betty was getting supper, and Joe was sitting in the living room reading the newspaper. Sambo was sleeping on the front porch when he heard a noise. He opened his eyes and saw the two dogs running right at him. Sambo did not have time to run and jump on the car. He jumped out of the way just as the largest dog jumped at him.

The large dog slid past Sambo, crashed through the glass of the front door, tumbled across the carpet, and smashed into Joe's lap. He yelped and ran back out through the broken door. The dog did not stop running until he crawled through the hole under the back yard fence. The other dog crawled under the fence right behind him.

"That does it!" Joe shouted. He threw down his newspaper. "Betty, I'm going over to the neighbor's house and tell him to keep his dogs penned up," Joe said. He walked over to the blue house and knocked on the front door.

Mr. Smith came to the door.

"I'm tired of your dogs coming into our yard," Joe said. "They pick on Sambo and Sambo jumps on our car to get away from them. Our new car has scratches all over it. Just now, your largest dog started chasing Sambo and crashed through our glass storm door," Joe explained.

"I'm terribly sorry," Mr. Smith replied. "I thought my dogs were penned up inside my back yard fence," he said.

"Come with me and I'll show you something," Joe said. He led Mr. Smith to the alley and showed him the place where the dogs had dug their way to freedom.

"Thank you for showing me the tunnel, Mr. Smith said. "I couldn't see it from inside the yard because some bushes were in front of it," he explained. "Show me your broken storm door and I will pay someone to fix it for you," the neighbor said.

The door was soon repaired. Mr. Smith put a piece of metal plate under the fence and filled the hole back up with dirt. The dogs tried and tried to dig out again, but the metal plate would not move.

Sambo was safe. He did not have to jump on the car anymore. Sambo took peaceful naps now, without feeling afraid. He started to enjoy living in town and only barked when some one walked up to the house.

Two years later Joe's father had a stroke and had to go to the hospital. Later, he was put into a Nursing Home. Betty and Joe moved to the south farm. They moved Betty's mobile home close to the Nursing Home for Joe's mother to live in.

Sambo now had a larger farm to protect and he worked hard to keep people away from the farm. He often killed rabbits and cats if he caught them too close to the farm house. Sambo barked at skunks and watched the cattle pens day and night in order to bark when the cattle were out.

One day Sambo barked at a rattle snake. The rattle snake did not crawl away. He took one long strike and one fang went into Sambo's leg. Sambo's leg begain to swell. He didn't feel well so he went to sleep on the back porch.

"What's the matter with Sambo?" Betty asked. "I can't wake him up!" she exclaimed.

Joe came running from the kitchen. He shook Sambo several times. "His foot is swollen!" Joe shouted. "Sambo has been bitten by a poison rattle snake!" he exclaimed. Joe carefully laid Sambo in the back seat of the car.

Betty jumped in the other side of the car and they were soon traveling fast to the animal hospital.

Sambo didn't move.

It took thirty minutes to reach the animal hospital. Joe picked up Sambo and carried him into the emergency room. "My dog has been bitten by a rattle snake!" Joe yelled.

The vet checked Sambo's leg and gave him several shots. He cut Sambo's leg and drained off some of the poison. "It's bad," the vet said.

Joe and Betty were sad. "We will call you tomorrow morning to see how Sambo is doing," Joe said.

The next morning Joe was afraid that Sambo might be dead and was almost afraid to call. He prayed before he picked up the telephone and dialed the vet's number. "How is Sambo?" he asked.

"He's doing great!" the vet exclaimed. "He woke up and is walking around on three legs. I think the worst is over," he said with a sigh. "You can come and pick him up tomorrow."

Sambo did not remember why he felt so weak. He did not know where he was, but the man was nice to him. Sambo was not afraid of this nice man.

Sambo slept most of the first day. He was glad when Joe and Betty came after him.

Joe and Betty hugged Sambo's neck. "You are a hero," Joe said. "If that snake had gotten into the yard, he might have bitten one of us," he explained.

"Sambo, you do a great job protecting our farm," Betty said and hugged Sambo's neck again. Sambo felt proud.

Betty was looking for eggs in an old storage building one evening when she heard a strange noise. Betty jumped because she remembered the rattle snake. "That sounds more like a mouse than a snake," Betty said.

Betty heard the noise again. "That doesn't sound like a mouse," Betty said. She started looking for what was making the noise. She decided that the funny noises were coming from under an old refrigerator that was stored in the building. Betty looked around for snakes, then she got down on her hands and knees and looked under the old refrigerator. She saw a round ball of gray fur.

Betty carefully put her fingers around the furry animal and gently pulled it out from under the refrigerator. It was a tiny, tabby-marked kitten. "I guess your mother was one of the wild cats that Sambo didn't see," she said. The kitten was so thin that Betty could see its tiny ribs.

Sambo wanted to see what Betty had found, but she took it to the house where it would be safe. Betty fed the kitten some warm milk. She named the kitten Tommy.

Tommy soon grew into a large tom cat, but Betty never let Tommy out of the house. She knew Sambo would chase Tommy, and Tommy might not get away. Tommy was happy just living in the large farm house.

One day Betty was not at home. Tommy was scratching around in a clay pot where one of Betty's large house plants was growing. He bit one of the large leaves. It tasted a little strange and Tommy ate most of the leaf. He felt like running and jumping.

That afternoon, when Betty came home from work, she found Tommy swinging on the macramé' table. "Tommy, what are you doing on that table?" Betty yelled.

Tommy looked at Betty. He jumped off the table, and ran into the large bedroom. Betty could not believe her eyes when she saw Tommy jump from the floor on one side of the bed, to the floor on the other side of the king-sized bed. "It's impossible for a cat to jump that far, and it looked like you were flying!" Betty exclaimed. "What's wrong with you?" she asked.

Tommy looked at Betty and tipped his head from side to side. Betty almost thought she saw the cat smile.

Suddenly, Tommy did not feel well. He crawled under the bed with a stomach ache. He stayed under the bed until the next morning.

Outside, Sambo was resting in his usual place and watching the road. His ears stood up as he heard a large vehicle coming down the road. He started barking at the truck as he watched it pull in behind the house. The truck parked beside the cow pens. The driver tried several times to back up the large truck to the cattle shoot.

Joe came out of the house and walked over to the large truck. "Would you like for me to back the truck and trailer up to the cattle shoot for you?" he asked. "It's pretty tricky to do if you're not used to it," he explained.

"I guess so," the driver answered, feeling a little embarrassed.

Joe pulled the truck forward. He backed the truck so that the large stock trailer pushed against the loading shoot of the cattle pens.

Sambo was still barking. He suddenly stopped barking and listened. He thought he heard barking coming back at him from the cab of the truck. Sambo backed up when he heard the barking again.

Joe stepped down from the large truck. "That's a nice looking Blue-Healer dog you have with you," he said. "Is she a cow dog?" Joe asked.

"She's supposed to be, the truck driver answered. "My dad was loading cattle this morning and dog was trying to help. She seemed to be doing everything wrong. Instead of barking the cattle in the right direction, she seemed to be scattering them. My dad got so mad at her that he told me to take her with me today and not to bring her back," the driver explained. "He didn't say so, but I think he intended for me to shoot her somewhere along the way."

"I don't want you to shoot her," Joe replied. "I think we have enough room around this farm for another dog. Sambo might like some company."

"I guess you can have her. I didn't want to shoot her anyway," the driver said. "What are you going to name her?" he asked.

"Well, she's lucky you came by here before you shot her," Joe replied. "I guess I'll call her Lucky."

Joe lifted Lucky down from the large truck. He patted the dog and put her down beside Sambo.

Sambo was embarrassed and ran under the house.

Lucky stayed close to Joe and helped Joe and the truck-driver load the cattle that were going to new pastures. The truck drove away from the farm, and Joe followed the truck in his pickup.

Lucky watched the vehicles leave the farm, and then she started to explore her new home. She looked in and around several buildings before she went to look for Sambo. Sambo was still hiding under the furthermost corner of the house. Lucky was much smaller than Sambo. She was able to crawl under the house easier than Sambo.

Lucky crawled up to Sambo and begin to lick him in the face.

Sambo tried to back up, but he was already against the cement foundation of the house. He could not move. Sambo soon overcame his fear of the strange dog and followed Lucky out from under the house. They were soon having a lot of fun chasing each other and running all around the farm together.

Sambo thought Lucky would help him with some of the work around the farm. He needed help guarding the place from intruders. Sambo soon knew that Lucky was not a guard dog. She seldom barked, and she was friendly with every people person that came to the farm.

Lucky was not pretty like Sambo. She was white with black splashes all over her. She looked like someone had dropped a bucket of white paint and it splattered all over her body. Lucky had a long nose. She was skinny, but she had large chest muscles.

The first day Lucky was on the farm, she caught a rabbit for her and Sambo to eat. Sambo loved the taste of fresh meat. Sambo had never seen a dog run as fast as Lucky; not even the two dogs in town.

One night the coyotes were howling close to the house. Sambo barked for a little while. The coyotes were coming closer. Sambo crawled back under the house. He waited for Lucky to follow him. Lucky stayed out in the yard and started to answer the coyote's yelp with yelps of her own. Sambo was sad when he saw Lucky trot down the road. He knew she was joining the coyotes.

Sambo missed Lucky so much that he would not eat. He only came out from under the house for a drink of water. Sambo walked around slowly with his tail between his legs. "I was never lonely before Lucky came here," Sambo told himself. "Why do I miss her so much now?" he asked himself.

Betty and Joe tried to get Sambo to eat, but he even refused the raw hamburger they brought him. He even turned down the scramble eggs, which was his favorite food.

"I'm afraid that Sambo is going to die," Betty said.

"If he doesn't start eating by Thursday, I'll take him back to the vet," Joe said.

Lucky was missing for several days. Sambo was now skinnier than Lucky.

Sambo was trying to sleep under the house one evening. Joe and Betty were walking back from the cattle pens where they had been feeding some calves. It was almost sundown. The coyotes begin to howl.

Sambo did not care to bark at the coyotes anymore. He heard the coyotes yelping, but his ears stood straight up when he heard a different yelp. It seemed to be getting closer. Sambo crawled out from under the house. He ran to the road where Joe and Betty were standing.

Sambo saw Lucky coming down the road toward the farm. The coyotes yelped and Lucky answered them. This happened over and over until Lucky was safely in the yard, then the coyotes were silent.

I wouldn't believe it if I hadn't seen it!" Joe exclaimed.

"Me either; the coyotes must be Lucky friends," Betty said.

"Maybe they let her run with them because she is such a good hunter," Joe said. "My mother's dog used to run with the coyotes. That's why we know that Sambo is half coyote, and looks more like a coyote than he looks like a dog. Some people have even shot at him and he has a bullet hole in one of his ears," he explained.

"I wondered why one ear looks different," Betty replied.

Sambo did not care what he was. He did not care where Lucky had been. All that was important was that Lucky was home again. He felt happy and hungry.

Lucky begin to lick Sambo in the face. They enjoyed a special meal that Betty fixed for them.

A few weeks later Lucky left with the coyotes again. This time Sambo was not sad. He knew that Lucky would come back.

Lucky begin to get fat. She was soon fatter than Sambo. Lucky's belly was soon the largest part of her. Sambo knew something exciting was getting ready to happen, and he could not understand why Lucky was so cranky.

CHAPTER 11

Puppies

It was a cold, early morning in March. Joe and Betty had heard Lucky crying under the house all night. Sambo knew that Lucky was hurting, but he did not know what to do to help her.

Suddenly, Lucky ran to the back door. When Betty opened the door, Lucky ran into the large bedroom and jumped up into a large, soft, bean-bag chair. She turned this way and that way, but she could not get comfortable.

"Joe, you need to fix Lucky a box with soft rags in it," Betty said. "I don't want Lucky to have her babies in my red velvet chair!" she exclaimed.

Joe got out of bed and found a large box in the garage. He filled it with rags and placed the box in the utility room. He placed Lucky in the box.

Lucky jumped out of the box and ran out of the house. She ran around and around the house before she returned to the box to rest.

"I have to go to work, now," Betty said. "Joe, I want you to call me when the puppies are born," she said. Betty patted Lucky on the head and left the house.

Sambo felt so confused that he crawled back under the house.

Betty worried about Lucky all morning. Lucky was so much smaller than the coyotes and Sambo. "I hope that Lucky's puppies are not too large to be born," Betty told herself. She called Joe during her morning coffee break. "Is Lucky okay and has she had any puppies yet?" Betty asked.

"She has one puppy. It's pretty big, and it's mostly black," Joe answered.

"Well, that doesn't sound like a coyote color. I guess Sambo is a proud daddy now," Betty replied.

"Lucky is having a hard time, but she seems to know what to do to help the pups to be born," Joe said.

That evening when Betty came home from work, there were two more puppies. Two of the pups were black with white chests, large fluffy tails, and brown feet. One of the pups looked just like Sambo. Betty and Joe thought the pup was probably half coyote just like Sambo.

Sambo came into the house and looked into the box where Lucky was feeding her puppies. He felt so happy and proud. Suddenly, Lucky jumped out of the box and caught him by the neck. She started to shake him like she was killing a rat.

When Lucky let go, Sambo ran out of the house, around the house, and crawled back under the house.

From then on, Sambo did not get close to the pups until they were almost grown.

"What are you going to name the pups?" Joe asked Betty.

"We'll just have to call this one Little Sambo," Betty said, lifting the coyote-looking pup out of the box. She patted the little ball of fur and put him back beside Lucky.

Betty picked up the smallest black pup. "This one has markings that look like rings above his eyes. He cries more than the others. I' think we'll call him Dingo," Betty said. She put the second pup back into the box beside Lucky.

Betty picked up the largest black puppy. I guess you'll have to name this one," she said.

"I'm not good at that kind of thing," Joe replied.

"Well, he's so much fun, let's call him Bingo," Betty said.

The puppies were now two weeks old. Lucky and her pups were still in the laundry room. One night Lucky wanted to go outside. The door was locked and Joe and Betty were in bed, asleep. Lucky tried and tried to get outside. She tore the wooden trim off from around the door. She scratched and scratched on the door, but she could not get out.

Betty found the damage the next morning. She decided that the puppies were old enough to be outside since their eyes were open. Betty took the box with the puppies inside and placed it in an old building north of the house. The building had once been a bunkhouse for ranch hands.

Betty put the box next to the south door and left the door open. Lucky could now come and go when she needed to. The southern sun warmed up the box during the day, and Lucky could keep the puppies warm at night.

Lucky was a good mother. She fed her puppies so much that they soon became fat, round, little balls of fur.

The puppies were soon able to crawl out of the box. Bingo crawled out of the box first. Dingo and Little Sambo cried and cried for Bingo. Two days later, Dingo and Little Sambo crawled out of the box trying to follow Bingo.

Bingo was always busy. He teased the other puppies by pulling their tails and ears. Bingo explored every corner of the two room old louse. One Day Bingo was sniffing the dust around the box. He waddled too close to the open door and fell out of the old building.

Dingo and Little Sambo cried for Bingo, but Bingo was not afraid. He tried to climb up the step. It was too tall for him. Bingo crawled under the edge of the old building and waited for Lucky, or Betty to find him. He watched a bug digging a hole under the old building.

Lucky found Bingo the first time he fell out of the door. She carefully picked him up with her teeth and put him back into the box.

Betty found Bingo under the building the next day. Bingo was soon too fat to crawl under the building, but the days were getting warmer now. Bingo was not cold anymore while he waited to be rescued.

One evening Betty checked on the puppies. Bingo was crying. "Bingo, I've never heard you cry before," Betty said. She picked Bingo up from the box. Bingo cried louder. "I know you're sick. I'm going to take you to the house with me," Betty said. She put her arms around Bingo and took him to the farm house.

Bingo

Little Sambo

Dingo

"Bingo has a stomach ache," Betty told Joe. She sat down in a rocking chair and rocked the sick puppy. Betty patted Bingo on the back just like she was burping a tiny baby. Bingo was still crying.

Joe looked worried for a minute before he exclaimed, "I have an idea!"

"What is it?" Betty asked.

"Let's give Bingo some aloe Vera juice. That's what we take when our stomach hurts," Joe explained.

"But, aloe Vera juice is for people, not dogs!" Betty replied.

"Well, it sure won't hurt him, and it might make him feel better," Joe said. He went to the refrigerator and got a bottle aloe juice. He went over to the cabinet and found a teaspoon. Joe came back into the living room where Betty was rocking Bingo.

Betty turned Bingo over on his back and propped his mouth open.

Joe filled the teaspoon with juice and poured it down Bingo's throat while Betty held him.

Betty put Bingo over her shoulder and started patting him again.

Bingo let out a large burp. He snuggled up to Betty's neck and went to sleep.

"See, it worked," Joe said with a smile.

Bingo has a stomach ache!

Lucky
Chasing rabbits
on the farm

CHAPTER III

Lucky is Boss

Lucky was a protective mother. She was afraid that even Sambo might hurt her puppies. Sambo weighed two times more than Lucky, but if Sambo came into the same area of the yard as the puppies, Lucky would start growling. If Sambo didn't run, Lucky would grab him by the neck again and shake him like she killed rabbits.

Sambo was so afraid that he spent most of his time still under the house. When someone came to the farm, Sambo had to bark at them from under the house. Sambo only came out from under the house when Betty called him to eat. If Lucky had been cranky that day, Sambo would not even come out to eat. Sambo grew thin again.

As the puppies grew older, Lucky was not so mean.

Sambo came out from under the house one day. He was walking around the farmyard when Little Sambo came up to him. Sambo wanted to play with his son, but he was still afraid of Lucky. Sambo just dropped his head and sadly walked away.

Little Sambo followed Big Sambo most of that day, and most of the time after that.

Lucky killed skunks and rats to protect her babies. She nursed her puppies until they were as large as she was. Finally, it was time to wean her babies. Lucky was thin. She snapped at the pups when they tried to get their dinner from her. It took the puppies two days to leave Lucky alone.

Lucky knew her growing family needed a lot to eat. Betty was now giving the pupies puppy dog food. Lucky begin to kill rabbits again, and she taught her sons to eat fresh meat. Sometimes, she even let Sambo join them for dinner.

Little Sambo grew thin like Big Sambo. Sambo tried to ignore Little Sambo, but the puppy followed Big Sambo everywhere. He even followed him under the house.

Bingo and Dingo looked like twins except Dingo had white fur around his nose. Bingo was taller and had large muscles like Lucky's. Both pups had large brown feet and legs. Their ears stood up straight and pretty like a German Shephard's ears.

All the pups had large furry tails. Bingo and Dingo's tails were black with white fur at the end of their tails.

Although the pups were larger than Lucky, she still pinned them down every day and gave each of them a bath.

The lamas spit on the students.

CHAPTER IV
Visiting school

It was almost time for summer vacation at the school where Betty taught sixth grade. The Science teacher was helping the fifth and sixth grade students plan their annual Science Animal Fair.

"Now remember class, the Fair will be the day before the last day of school, and I want each of you to bring your pets and any other animals you might want to show the other students," Mrs. Hefley said.

"Can we bring large animals too?" asked Gary.

"Sure, Mrs. Hefley answered. "If they are too large to come into our classroom, you can keep them in your horse trailers on the south side the classroom door," she explained.

The big day finally came. All the students brought their pets and animals. There were some real large dogs. One girl brought a litter of tiny, white, angora kittens.

One boy brought two lamas. When the students stood too close to the lamas, the lamas spit on the students. At first the students were frightened, but they thought it was funny when the lamas spit on someone else.

A few students brought their riding ponies. One trailer had two deer in it. Some students brought pet rabbits and kittens. A few students brought pet chickens. The school yard looked like a horse show with all the trailers parked around the Science room door.

Betty brought Bingo, Dingo, and Little Sambo. The pups were the most popular animals at the fair. Although the pups were pretty heavy by this time, the students carried them around all day. Betty checked on the pups once when all the students were outside in PE class. Bingo, Little Sambo, and Dingo were asleep on the hardwood floor of the Science room. "You poor babies. You must be very tired," Betty whispered. She closed the door and hurried back to her own class to finish her Math lesson.

After PE, the students were dismissed to spend the rest of the day with the animals. Robin carried Bingo up to Betty, and asked, "Teacher, would you please give Bingo to me?"

"Oh dear, what would your mother say if you came home with a puppy without asking her first?" Betty asked.

"She wouldn't care because she loves dogs," Robin said.

"I didn't bring Bingo to school to give him away," Betty replied. "My husband would be sad if I have Bingo away."

Robin looked disappointed and carried Bingo back outside. Jack took Bingo from Robin and carried him around the animal trailers. He came over to where Betty was standing. "Would you please give Bingo to me?" Jack asked.

"Oh dear, what would your mother say if you came home with a puppy without asking her first?" Betty asked Jack.

"She would be happy. She loves dogs, and Bingo is such a pretty dog," Jack answered.

"I didn't bring Bingo to school to give him away," Betty said. "My husband would be sad if I gave Bingo away," she explained again.

Jack looked disappointed and walked away. Shawn took Bingo from Jack and carried him around. Bingo kissed Shawn on the neck. Shawn walked over to Betty. "Teacher, would you give Bingo to me, please," Shawn begged.

"Oh dear, what would your mother say if you brought a new dog home without asking?" Betty asked.

"She wouldn't care. She likes dogs," Shawn answered.

"I didn't bring Bingo to school to give him away," Betty replied. "Besides, my husband would be very sad if I gave Bingo away," she explained for the third time.

"But, you have two other dogs," Shawn said.

"We love each of the puppies and don't want to give them away right now," Betty tried to explain.

Bingo kissed each student that carried him. It seemed that every student wanted Bingo. Betty was glad that Bingo was so popular, but she was almost sorry she had brought him to school.

Robin asked for Bingo two more times before he gave up. "I know why you named him Bingo, Robin said.

"Why do you think we named him Bingo?" Betty asked.

"Because he's a winner, and he will always be a winner," Robin answered.

"I think you're right," Betty replied.

The day was soon over and the parents came after the animals. Betty told her students good-bye and put the puppies in the car. She went back to her school room to check everything, turn off the lights, and lock the door. Betty, Bingo, Dingo, and Little Sambo were soon going over the bumpy dirt road toward the farm. The pups were so glad to get home that they ran all over the farm yard.

Bingo was the most popular animal at the animal fair!

CHAPTER V
Summer

The winter snow storms had killed a lot of cattle and destroyed many of the fall crops. Joe and Betty lost so much money on the farm that they had to quit farming. They sold the cattle that hadn't died in the snow storms, and the bank took ownership of the land. Joe found a job working for a heath product company. The company needed Joe to travel and sell products.

When school was out for the summer, Betty went with Joe on his business trips. Sometimes Joe and Betty were gone for a week. They could not take the five dogs with them, but they left plenty of dog food for the dogs. Joe left one water hose slightly turned on over a large pan. The dogs always had fresh water to drink. The dogs were never hungry or thirsty, but they were lonely.

Sambo worked extra hard to protect the farm now. Little Sambo helped Big Sambo bark at all the intruders that came close to the farm yard. They barked at skunks, rats, cats, birds, and people.

Lucky, Bingo, and Dingo were too friendly to people to be much help in protecting the farm. Sambo was glad for Little Sambo's help.

While the two Sambos protected the farm, Lucky hunted for mice and rabbits to give her family fresh meat to eat.

Some afternoons the five dogs lay close to the road and listened for Joe and Betty to come home. Sometimes they wondered if Joe and Betty would ever come home again. The dogs were always excited when they finally saw Joe and Betty's van coming down the road.

All five dogs ran to meet Joe and Betty. It was hard for Joe and Betty to get into the house with the dogs jumping up on them and kissing them. Sambo and Lucky stayed outside, but the three pups ran through the house until they were panting.

The pups each weighed over fifty pounds now. They sounded like bears loping across the floor. One by one they tried to jump on Betty's lap, but they were so big that they fell off of Betty's lap and landed back on the floor.

Joe and Betty were looking through their week's mail. Bingo, Dingo, and Little Sambo put their front paws on the kitchen table and it looked like they were looking through the mail, too. They looked at the letters, turning their heads from side to side. They were trying to figure out the meaning of all the papers.

"Betty, we're going to have to move away from the farm and move to the city," Joe said.

"Oh, Jo, do we have to?" Betty asked.

"Yes Betty. The bank now owns the farm and it will soon be sold to another farmer. We need to be in the city for our new business," Joe answered.

"We can't take all the dogs with us," Betty said. She felt sad. "What are we going to do?" she asked.

"I have decided to take Dingo to my aunts," Joe said. "She has a pretty farm where he can play. I know Dingo will be happy there," Joe explained.

Joe and Betty took Dingo to Aunt Claire's the next day. They told Dingo good-bye. On the way home, Joe stopped by his cousin's farm. "Henry, could you use another cow dog around here?" Joe asked.

"Yes," said Henry. "My son is looking for a pup, too, to train to work with cattle," Cousin Henry said.

Betty and Joe went back to the farm and loaded Lucky to take to Cousin Henry's. But, which pup would they give to Henry's son?

"I hate to give Little Sambo away because he looks like a coyote just like Big Sambo," Joe said.

"I know, but I love Bingo too much to give him away," Betty said. She hugged Bingo's large neck.

"Me too," Joe said. "We just can't give Bingo, the winner away."

Joe and Betty put Little Sambo in the pickup beside Lucky. They drove the fifteen miles back to Henry's place. "Thank you for taking these dogs," Joe said. "I know you'll take good care of them."

Betty and Joe told Lucky and Little Sambo good-bye for the last time. They felt sad. Betty almost cried when only Sambo and Bingo were at the farm to meet them when they drove up to the farmhouse.

The next week when Joe and Betty came back to the farm, Joe was driving a large U-Haul truck. Sambo and Bingo watched Joe and Betty load the truck with all the furniture from the large house. Betty loaded their best clothes in the back of the van. Joe lifted Sambo, then Bingo, into the van.

Bingo had never ridden in a large vehicle before. He was a little frightened at first. Bingo finally stretched out on the back seat and went to sleep. Sambo lay down close to Betty's seat. Betty followed the U-Haul truck down the dusty road.

Sambo tried to look through the windshield for awhile. He barked at car lights that passed by. Sambo tried to crawl up into Betty's lap. "Stay down, Sambo, so I can see to drive," Betty had to tell Sambo, over and over.

Sambo finally lay down on the floor and went to sleep.

Joe and Betty stopped at a gas station to fill up both the U-Haul truck and the van. Sambo barked at the people he saw around the gas station. He was still trying to be a watchdog.

Joe and Betty put leashes on Sambo and Bingo's collars and walked them around the station. After the dogs had done their "business", Betty and Joe loaded them back into the van and continued driving toward the city.

It took six hours to get to the city. It was late at night when the van and U-Haul truck finally pulled into the driveway of their new home. The house that Joe and

Betty had rented was on a mountain above a large city.

Joe and Betty let the two dogs out of the van.

Sambo went to do his "business", but Bingo turned around and saw all the lights below him. He had never seen a city before. He had never been on a mountain before. Bingo just sat back, staring at all the bright lights below. His mouth was dropped open and his eyes were bugging out. The lights were so interesting that Bingo forgot to do his "business". Betty had to get up in the middle of the night to let Bingo back outside.

The two dogs ran into the garage and around the first floor of the house. They ran up the stairs that led to the main floor of the large house. Sambo and Bingo ran through each room until they were familiar with the whole house.

Joe and Betty set up one bed down stairs. They put sheets and blankets on it, and then they called the dogs. After the dogs had eaten some dog food and drank a lot of water, they were ready to rest. Sambo lay down on Joe's side of the bed. Bingo lay down on Betty's side of the bed. Betty, Joe, Sambo, and Bingo were soon asleep.

CHAPTER VI

Living in the City

The next morning Joe and Betty let the dogs outside. Sambo and Bingo ran around the house and explored the large yard on the mountain top.

Betty called the dogs back inside and gave them more dog food and water. While the dogs ate, Joe and Betty drove down the mountain to a nearby restaurant to eat breakfast. Later, the dogs played in the yard while Joe and Betty unloaded the furniture.

Sambo laid down to rest. Bingo lay down beside Sambo. Bingo saw a strange white thing in the yard next door. He did not know it was a newspaper. Bingo ran into the neighbor's yard and grabbed the newspaper. He tossed it into the air.

The newspaper landed with a thud and bounced. The rubber band broke and the newspaper landed flat on the grass.

Bingo jumped on the white paper that was moving with the wind. The paper tore. Pieces of paper floated up into the air. Bingo watched the paper floating in the wind and tore off more pieces. Soon the newspaper was scattered all over the yard.

Bingo lay down beside Sambo again and rested. He noticed another newspaper in the yard across the street. Bingo ran over across the street and picked up the newspaper with his teeth. He tossed the newspaper into the air. The rubber band did not break this time. Bingo used his claws to pull at the rubber band. He worked and worked until the band broke. Bingo tore pieces off of the paper and watched the wind blow them down the street. The paper was soon blowing all over the street and yard.

Tearing the paper was so much fun that Bingo ran into every yard on the street and tore up each newspaper. Bingo felt tired and was resting beside Sambo when Betty walked out onto the porch.

"Oh no!" Betty exclaimed when she saw the torn newspapers everywhere. "Joe, come here quick!" Betty yelled.

"Bingo, you made a terrible mess, bad dog!" Betty shouted.

Bingo put his tail between his legs and ran under the back porch.

Betty went back into the house and pulled a large trash bag out of a kitchen drawer. She picked up pieces of newspaper for the rest of the morning.

Joe went to the house next door. He rang the doorbell. No one answered. Joe rang the bell several more times. "I guess no one is home," he said.

Joe went to the next house. He rang the doorbell. Joe rang the bell again. This time a little, elderly woman came to the door. "Excuse me Mam, but I have to tell you that my dog tore up your newspaper this morning," Joe explained. "I'm very sorry."

"That's awful!" the woman exclaimed. "If you don't keep your dog in your yard, I'm going to call the police."

"I'm going to tie him up from now on," Joe said. "We just moved to the city from the farm, and I guess my dog is still a little bit country."

"I think he's a little wild, if you ask me," the woman said and slammed the door shut.

Joe went to every house on both sides of the street. He rang every door bell. Joe felt relieved that so many people were not at home, and he didn't have to apologize to everyone. Most of the people that were home just laughed at what Bingo had done. A few people were mad because they could not read their newspaper that day.

Betty felt embarrassed while she was picking up pieces of paper from her new neighbor's yards. She was glad that no one came out of the houses and asked her what she was doing in their yard.

Joe walked up the steps and into the house. Bingo followed him to the large storage room downstairs.

Joe looked through some boxes until he found a long chain that he had brought from the farm. "I hate to do this to you, boy, but I have to," Joe said. He put the chain around Bingo's collar and snapped it tight.

Bingo followed Joe outside. He did not know that he would have be where the chain pulled him.

Joe put the other end of the chain around one of the poles on the back porch and walked back into the house.

Bingo followed Joe across the yard. Suddenly, something stopped him so quickly that he fell backwards. Bingo struggled to his feet and tried again. The chain would not let him go any farther. Bingo lay down and cried. "There must be some way I can get away from this thing," Bingo told himself. He started chewing on the chain.

Sambo saw someone walking down the street and started barking. He ran to the edge of the yard and barked at the man. The man walked quickly past the yard. "I don't need to bark anymore," Sambo thought. He lay down on the front porch to take another nap. "It's hard to guard this place with so many people around," Sambo told himself with a sigh.

Bingo was still chewing on his chain. He heard a loud click and jumped. The chain dropped from his collar. "I'm free!" Bingo told himself. He was so happy that he ran from one side of the yard to the other, and back again.

Joe noticed that Bingo was loose. He came out of the house and tied Bingo to the pole again. "Bingo, you have to stay in our yard or we'll be in big trouble," Joe said. He patted Bingo on the head and went back into the house.

Sambo had always lived outside and the house was too worm for him. He was glad when Betty and Joe started letting him sleep on the front porch all night. Sambo knew where the yard ended, even without a fence. He never ran out of the yard and Joe did not have to tie up Sambo.

It was still dark when Sambo saw someone walking down the street. "I must guard Joe and Betty," Sambo barked. He ran into the street and barked his loudest bark.

The boy stood still in the street. Sambo was frightened so he started to growl. The boy turned and ran into the nearest yard.

Sambo's barking had awakened Joe and Betty. They put on their robes and ran to the front windows. "I see someone out there," Betty said. "I think it's a man," she said.

"He acts like he want to come up to our house, but Sambo is keeping him away," Joe said.

The person disappeared. Several minutes later the telephone rang. "Your dog won't let me deliver your newspaper, or anyone's paper, this morning," a young voice said. "You better come and get him or no one will get their paper today."

Joe ran out of the house and called Sambo. Sambo had to stay in the house.

The paper boy came out of the neighbor's house. Joe watched the lights in the house go off. The people were probably going back to bed. Joe took his newspaper from the paper boy. "I'm sorry about Sambo scaring you, and I'll be sure he doesn't bother you again," Joe said.

"Be sure that you do," the paper boy said. "I don't have time to slow down when I'm on my paper route."

Joe went back to bed with the two dogs lying beside the bed. Betty was already asleep again.

The sun was soon shining. Joe went back to the storage room and found another long chain for Sambo.

He took both dogs outside and chained them to the back porch.

Sambo lay down on the porch. It did not bother him to be chained to the pole.

Bingo tried to follow Joe again. Again, the chain jerked him back. Bingo fell. He rolled over and started chewing on his chain again. The chain would not open. Bingo ran as far as the chain would let him run in one direction, then he ran the length of the chain in the other direction. Bingo could not get free.

Bingo ran the length of the chain again. This time he ran back to the porch on the other side of the large light pole in the back yard. This made his chain shorter. Bingo had just enough chain left to jump up on the railing of the porch. He was still fighting with his chain when he accidentally fell of the opposite side of the railing. There was not enough chain for Bingo paws to touch the ground. The collar tightened around his neck. Bingo could not breathe. He used the air that was left in his lungs to yelp for the last time.

Betty was looking out of the window. "Oh no, Bingo has hung himself!" Betty shouted. She ran out of the house. Joe was running right behind her.

"I wish Bingo would stop all that noise," Sambo thought when Bingo was running everywhere. Sambo heard more noises. He was angry. He ran over to where Bingo was hanging and bit one of his hind legs. This scared Bingo. He leaped into the air, landed back on the porch rail, and un-hung himself.

Joe and Betty watched Bingo unhang himself. "Thanks, Sambo, we couldn't get here in time to save him," Joe said.

Bingo looked embarrassed. He put his tail between his legs and crawled under the porch again.

Bingo hated his chain. He chewed on it the next morning until it unlatched from his collar. Bingo was free, but he did not run around the yard while Joe was watching.

Betty was doing the breakfast dishes. She was watching several children standing in line on the sidewalk on the other side of the street. They were waiting for the school bus. Suddenly, Betty saw something in the line. It was not a child. It was Bingo. The children were hugging Bingo and he was kissing them. "It almost looks like Bingo is keeping them warm on this chilly morning on the mountain," Betty said.

The telephone rang and Betty forgot about Bingo. When Betty hung up the telephone, she went outside to check on Bingo. Bingo was lying on the front porch. He was holding his head up, proudly. Under his front paws was a small child's coat.

"Oh Bingo, how could you?! Betty asked. "Joe, come here," Betty called.

Joe came outside and chained Bingo to the back porch pole again. He took the coat to every house on the street. He asked every person if the coat belonged to their child. Most of the neighbors were not at home. Those that were home did not recognize the coat. Joe finally took the coat back home.

It was almost dark that evening when the doorbell rang. Joe answered the door.

"May I have my coat back please, mister," a small boy asked.

Joe handed the lad the coat. "I'm sorry my dog took your coat," Joe said.

The boy shook his head and ran back across the street.

The next day Betty was visiting with one of the neighbors.

The neighbor saw Bingo and said, "That sure is a beautiful dog you have."

"We think he's pretty, and he just loves kids," Betty replied.

Bingo stood up.

The neighbor noticed how large Bingo was. "Does he like kids with salt and pepper?" the neighbor asked with a laugh.

CHAPTER VIII
The dog-napping

"Betty, I want you to go back to the farm and watch the Simpsons harvest our last milo crop," Joe said.

"Why do you want me to do that?" Betty asked.

"I want you to count the truck loads of grain that go to the grain elevator; I want to be sure the Simpsons pay us our share," Joe explained.

"They are our friends, Joe, and they wouldn't cheat us," said Betty.

"I need you to go and count the loads, anyway," Joe replied. "I would go, but I'm too busy."

"May I take Bingo with me?" Betty asked. "I think he might enjoy running around the old farm for a few days."

"That would be a good idea," Joe answered. "If anyone comes around the farm while you're there, Bingo can warn you by barking," he said. "You should be home by Thanksgiving. You can clean up that old trailer home we bought and see if it is anything we can use or sell."

Betty packed a suitcase with enough clothes to last a week. She put the suitcase in the van. Betty put a sack of dog food and a covered dish of water in the van, then she called for Bingo.

Bingo came running. Betty put Bingo into the van and he jumped up on the couch. Bingo stretched out and waited for a ride.

"I think he likes to travel," Betty said, laughing. She kissed Joe good-bye, and backed the van away from the large house.

Bingo jumped over the front seat. He put his front paws on the dash and watched the trees and cars go by as the van traveled down the mountain. Bingo watched the city traffic go by. So many cars going by made him sleepy. Betty was driving out of the city when Bingo jumped back into the back seat. He lay back down on the couch and was soon asleep.

Betty stopped at a gas station. She started the gas pump, and then she took Bingo out of the van. Bingo was so large and excited that he took Betty for a walk. He wanted to explore every area around the gas station. Betty pulled Bingo into a vacant lot next to the station. Bingo did his "business". On the way back to the van, Bingo got twisted up in his chain and broke three of Betty's fingernails.

"Bingo, don't get so excited," Betty said. She put Bingo back into the van and finished filling the van with gas. They were soon traveling back on the busy interstate highway, and Bingo was back on the couch sleeping in no time.

"Bingo, we're going to be staying with my son, Martin," Betty said.

Bingo sat up and leaned his head from side to side. He always did that when he was trying to figure out what Betty was saying. Bingo laid his head down again.

Betty drove four more hours. "Bingo, there's Washtown," she said.

Bingo raised his head to look at the lights of the small town.

"I think we'll go by Al and Wilma's house first," Betty said. It's still early, and I haven't seen my friends for a long time." Betty parked the van in front of her friends' house.

"I'll let you spend some time outside, Bingo," Betty said. She put the chain on Bingo's collar again and fastened the other end of the chain to the door handle of the van. "I'll see you in a little while," Betty said. She knocked on the front door of the house.

"Betty, what a surprise. Come on in," Wilma said.

Betty followed Wilma into the living room. Al stood up and shook hands with Betty. "It's been a long time since we've seen you," Al said. "How is life in the city?" he asked.

"It's very different from the farm, but we like it," Betty answered. She sat down in a large living room chair and visited with her friends.

Bingo was waiting beside the van when he decided to see how far his chain would let him run. Bingo ran to the back of the van and then he ran in front of the van. Bingo ran straight out to the edge of the street before the chain stopped him.

A pickup truck, with two men in it, was going down the street. "Hey, Charlie, look at that beautiful dog over there," one said.

"He is about the prettiest dog I've seen for a long time," Luke agreed.

"It makes me angry when I see a dog tied up like that!" Charley exclaimed. "I think anyone that ties up a dog doesn't deserve to have a dog."

"I agree with you; lets take him," Luke said.

"What if he tries to bite us?" Charlie answered.

"He looks friendly to me," said Luke. "Here doggie," the man said.

Bingo loved attention. He ran as close to the pickup truck as his chain would allow him. Bingo smiled and wagged his tail. The two men climbed out of the pickup truck. They were glad that Bingo kissed them instead of biting them. He didn't even bark. Charlie and Luke quickly unfastened Bingo's chain and Bingo followed them to the pickup truck.

"He sure is heavy," Luke whispered when he lifted Bingo into the seat of the pickup truck.

"Let's get out of here quick!" Charlie exclaimed. He climbed under the wheel of the vehicle and the two men quickly drove out of town.

Bingo sat tall between the two men and watched the road.

"Do you think we should have done this?" Charlie asked.

Sure, the people probably won't miss him for a long time, and we'll see that he's never tied up again," Luke answered.

"You asked me how we like the city," Betty said. "We really like living there, but it has been hard for

Sambo and Bingo to get used to living in the city," Betty explained. "Bingo has grown so much you might not recognize him." "Would you like to see him?" Betty asked.

"Sure," Al and Wilma both answered.

"He needs to spend a little more time outside, and then I'll go get him," Betty said. When she thought Bingo had been outside long enough, Betty went back to the van to get Bingo. The chain was still on the door handle, but Bingo and his collar were gone. "Bingo, here Bingo," Betty called.

There was only silence in the darkness. "Oh dear, Bingo has been stolen," Betty whispered. She ran back into the house. "Someone has stolen Bingo!" Betty yelled. "If he was close enough to hear me call him, he would come running." Betty felt like crying.

"Oh no, this town already has too many dogs, and nobody would want another one around here," Al said.

"But Bingo is a pretty dog!" Betty exclaimed.

Al and Wilma helped Betty look for Bingo. They looked up and down every street close by. They look and called until midnight.

"I need to go to Martin's house because it's so late," Betty said. "I'll look for him in the morning. It will be daylight then and easier to look for him."

It was cold, but Betty rolled down the Windows of the van and drove up and down every street in town. She called and whistled for Bingo until her voice was gone. Betty felt cold tears on her cheeks. She drove to Martin's house and quietly went downstairs and slipped into bed. Betty tried to get warm under the blankets while she used the downstairs phone, next to the bed, to call Joe.

"Joe, I have good news and bad news," Betty said.

"Give me the good news first," Joe answered.

"They are starting milo harvest tomorrow," Betty answered.

"What is the bad news?" Joe asked.

"Bingo has been dog-napped," Betty answered.

"That is bad news," Joe replied. "I sure hope you can find him. I sure would miss him if something happened to him."

"I miss him and I miss you, too," Betty said. She hung up the telephone and tried to go to sleep.

The two men took Bingo to a farm. Bingo jumped out of the pickup truck and looked for Betty. He ran around and around the pickup truck, but he was afraid to run anywhere else because it was dark.

"Come on boy and I'll feed you," Charlie said. "I have a lot of dog food left since my old dog died a few weeks ago. I sure hope you like it."

The dog food tasted strange to Bingo and he wasn't very hungry anyway. Instead of eating the dog food, Bingo followed the two men into the house. They walked through a porch and into a large kitchen. Charlie turned on the coffee pot while Luke took a package of cookies from a cabinet. The two men gave Bingo several pieces of their cookies. Luke put a bowl on the floor and filled it with water for Bingo.

Luke and Charley talked for awhile before they went to bed. Charlie went into one bedroom and Luke went into the other. "Which one of us are you going to sleep with?" Charlie asked Bingo.

Bingo thought Charlie petted him more than Luke did, so he followed Charlie and jumped up on his unmade bed. "I wish Betty would come here and get me," Bingo told himself as he went to sleep in this strange place.

It took Betty a long time to go to sleep. It seemed like she had just gone to sleep when she heard noises coming from upstairs. Betty opened her eyes. It was daylight. Betty heard her grandson running across the floor upstairs. She smelled bacon and eggs cooking on the stove. Betty jumped up and put on her old field clothes. She ran upstairs and greeted Martin, his wife Kasey, and grandson Bobby.

After everyone had said hello, the family sat down to eat breakfast, and Martin asked the blessing. Betty waited until everyone started to eat when she said, "Someone dog-napped Bingo last night."

Martin was on the city counsel. "Oh no, there are already too many dogs around this town. No one would want another dog around here!" he exclaimed.

"But Bingo is a pretty dog, and he just loves everyone," Betty tried to explain again.

Martin picked up the telephone and dialed the police. He handed the telephone to Betty.

"I want to report a missing dog," Betty said.

"How long has the dog been missing?" the police officer asked.

"Since about seven o'clock last night," Betty answered.

"I'll come to your house right away and write up a report," the policeman said. "Where do you live?" he asked.

"I don't live here, but I'm at my son's house now," Betty said. "He lives at 219 Elm Street."

"I'll be there as soon as possible," the officer replied.

Betty, and her family, finished eating breakfast. Martin and Kasey had left for work and Bobby had left for school, before the black police car drove up in front of the house. Betty opened the front door before the policeman could ring the doorbell. "Come on in," she said.

The policeman sat down at the dining room table. He motioned for Betty to sit next to him. "Now tell me what happened last night," the man said.

"I live in the city, but I came back here for milo harvest. I was visiting my friends over on Oak Street. I tied Bingo to the door handle of my van. I was not gone very long. When I came back to the van to get Bingo, he was not there. The chain was still on the door handle, but my dog was missing. I called and looked for him until midnight. I know someone has dog napped him, or he would come to me when I call him," Betty said.

"Oh no, I'm sure no one has stolen your dog. There are too many dogs in this town already, and I'm sure no one would want another one?" the policeman exclaimed.

"But, Bingo is a beautiful dog. He is friendly to everyone," Betty tried to explain again.

"Okay, okay, lady, I believe you," the police officer said. "Now tell me what kind of dog I'll be looking for."

"Bingo will soon be a year old. He weighs about sixty pounds. Bingo is black, with a white cross of fur on his chest. His feet are large and brown. Bingo's tail is long and fluffy, and his ears stand straight like a German

Shepherd's. He holds his head proudly. I think he looks like a show-dog," Betty answered.

"I can tell that you really love your dog," the policeman said. "I'll try to help you get your dog back."

Out in the country Charlie and Luke got up early. Bingo went with Luke out to feed some horses, pigs, and cats. The cats were not very friendly. Charlie had breakfast ready and on the table by the time Luke and Bingo came back into the house. Bingo ended up eating pancakes instead of dog food.

"We're going to check on cattle this morning, and I'm going to teach you how to be a cattle dog," Charley said.

"What are you going to name him?" Luke asked.

"By the way he holds his head high, I think I'll call him Prince," Charlie answered.

Bingo followed the two men on horses through the empty pen and out into the pasture. He felt so important.

"There's two of the yearlings we are taking to market," Charley said, "Go get em!" he yelled at Bingo.

Bingo ran toward the two steers.

Instead of running from him, one of the steers ran right at Bingo. The steer snorted at Bingo, and blew slobbers all over him.

Bingo ran as fast as could run. He ran to a fence and squeezed under it.

The steer bellowed at Bingo again before he ran to join the other steer.

Bingo lay on the ground afraid to move.

"I think you're going to have to work very hard to make a cattle dog out of Prince," Luke said, before he started laughing. He laughed so hard he almost fell off his horse.

Charlie did not say anything. He turned his horse around and rode after the two steers. Luke finally stopped laughing and joined Charlie. Together they drove the steers into one of the empty pens and went to look for more yearlings.

Bingo lay in the dirt a long time. He did not feel very cool. Bingo did not plan to move until Charlie came after him, but a large furry creature with six legs came walking toward him. The animal was so ugly that Bingo decided he better get out of the creature's way. He did not know it was a tarantula.

Bingo slipped back inside the fence to get away from the ugly bug. He stepped into a pile of something that smelled awful. Bingo started to clean off his feet with his tongue, but the brown stuff was too terrible. He rolled over and over in some loose dirt and tried to get the smell off his feet.

Bingo watched Luke and Charlie riding their horses from one side of the pasture to the other side. He shook as he thought of the large steer chasing him.

Bingo felt tired, hungry, thirsty, and lonesome. He wondered why Betty did not come and get him and take him home. Bingo wished he was lying on the cool grass in front of their home on the mountain. It was a long time before he was able to follow Luke and Charlie back to the house and get a drink.

After the police officer left, Betty crawled into the van. She drove up and down every street in town looking for Bingo. She called and whistled, but there was no sign of Bingo. Betty finally gave up and drove out to the old farm.

Betty opened the door of the old farmhouse and stepped back to get out of the dust that fell from the top of the door. She stepped into the house that she and Joe had lived in for four years. The house looked old, dirty, and empty.

Betty looked through the bedroom window that faced the field of milo. A combine was emptying milo into a farm truck. The truck backed out of the field and headed toward town. "I hope that is the first truck load of grain that has gone to grain elevator in town," Betty said to herself. "I hope I haven't missed counting any of the loads."

Betty took a piece of paper from her purse and taped it next to the front door. She put a mark on the paper representing a truckload of grain. Betty left the house and went to the back house to start cleaning out a small camper trailer that Tim had bought from an old woman. She opened the door and stepped back again to miss the falling dust.

The camper was so full of newspapers, magazines, and junk that Betty had no room to step inside. She reached for an armload of papers and took them to the old trash barrel. "I hope the wind doesn't start blowing before I get all this trash burned," Betty said to herself.

She found a small book of matches in her purse and lit one to start the paper burning. The paper burned easily and Betty went back for another load. She found a box full of magazines and emptied them into the fire. Betty used the box to carry more papers to the fire.

By noon, Betty had carried enough junk out of the tiny house that she was able to walk around in the tiny living room. She had three more marks for the loads of grain on the piece of paper. Betty stopped to rest and eat lunch.

Bingo stayed at the farm house and rested under the shade trees while Luke and Charlie rounded up cattle all afternoon. The pens west of the house were now full of yearling calves. Bingo thought the bellowing calves were too noisy and made it hard for him to take naps.

Luke and Charlie unsaddled their horses and put them out to pasture. "Let's go into town to eat supper and see what's going on there," Luke said.

"Sounds good to me, but what will we do with Prince while we're gone?" Charlie asked. "I don't think we should take him to town with us this quick in case someone is looking for him," he explained.

"Well, we can drive into Prairie Town instead," Luke said. "No one will be looking for Prince there, and it's only ten miles further away."

Bingo was glad to jump into the pickup truck between the two men and go for a ride. He was hoping he would see Betty. Bingo felt terribly bored with these two men. It was more fun living with Betty and Joe in the city. Bingo was eve bored staying in the truck waiting for Charlie and Luke to come back from the café.

Luke and Charlie smelled like people food when they crawled back into the truck. Charlie un-wrapped a napkin and gave Bingo some chicken bones. There were some good things about being with Luke and Charlie.

Bingo tried to sleep while he waited for Luke and Charlie to come back from the movie theater. The day had just been too long and boring. The men finally came back. Luke drove them home while Charlie talked to Bingo.

"When I have more time, boy, I'll teach you how to chase cattle rather than run from them" Charlie said, "I'll even teach you how to run them into pens and cattle trucks." Charley petted Bingo and gave him a hug.

Bingo was ready to go to sleep in front of the cool breeze coming through the window above Charlie's bed. Being bored all day had been very tiring. Bingo did not wake up until the next morning.

Betty had worked until dark and the combine across the field had stopped. She now had eight marks on her piece of paper. She felt a little creepy on the old farm, in the dark by herself, and was glad to crawl into the van and start back to town. "I sure wish Bingo were here with me," she said.

Betty drove up and down every street in town, again, calling for Bingo. She went to the police station to see if anyone there had seen Bingo.

"No mam, but we are still looking for him," a lady police officer said. "I really doubt if we find him since he has been missing for so long."

"I just can't give up looking for him, but thanks anyway," Betty said. She went back to Martin's for supper and a night's rest. "I sure hope Bingo doesn't freeze to death somewhere," Betty told Martin.

"The nights aren't that cold yet, and Bingo has a heavy coat of fur; it would be pretty hard for him to get too cold," Martin replied.

"I sure hope you're right," Betty sighed. She called Joe again that night to report on the progress of the harvest, cleaning the camper, and that Bingo was still missing.

"I sure hope you find Bingo before it's time for you to come home," Joe said again.

The second day went as slow as the first. Betty drove all over town again on her way to the farm calling for Bingo. She saw a lot of dogs, but none of them were as large and pretty as Bingo. She finally gave up and went on to the farm.

The combine stopped for about two hours during the day. Betty knew it had broken down and the Simpsons had to go somewhere after parts to fix it. There were only eight loads taken to the grain elevator that day.

Betty had cleaned out the junk in the bathroom of the camper and found that the fixtures needed to be replaced. It wasn't worth working on any longer. She was glad Joe only paid two-hundred dollars for the camper.

Once again, Betty was almost afraid to be on the farm alone after dark. She was glad when the harvesting stopped and she could go back to town. She checked all the streets calling for Bingo. Betty stopped by the police station again.

"I don't think we are going to find him," the friendly police officer said, "We won't stop looking for him, but

I imagine that someone picked him up and that they are hundreds of miles from here by now."

"I won't ever give up, but thanks," Betty said.

Betty had not been able to spend much time with her six-year-old grandson since they had moved to the city. She enjoyed the evenings watching Bobby run and play, listening to him read, and playing with him and the four kittens that were running around the house. The kittens made her miss Bingo even more.

The third morning Betty was ready to leave for the farm when she heard a car pull up to the house. She looked out and saw a policeman coming to the door. "Lady, I think I've found a friend of yours," he said.

Betty ran out to the patrol car. Bingo was sitting proudly in the middle of the back seat. His head was held high. He did not know that he was sitting where there were bars on the windows. He did not know that he was sitting where criminals usually ride.

"Oh Bingo, I'm so glad to see you," Betty said. She opened the car door and gave Bingo a hug. "Ugh, you smell like smoke and you need a bath," Betty said, laughing. "Thank you so much officer for finding my dog," Betty said. "But, how did you find him?" she asked.

"Well mam, I was driving down Main Street this morning when I saw a pickup with two men in it. I saw this large dog sitting between them. It caught my attention because most dogs around here ride in the back of the pickups.

I stopped the men, and saw that the dog fit the description you gave me. I called, 'Here Bingo', and the dog tried to come to me. I knew it was your dog mam.

I asked the men where they had gotten their dog. They said they found him in another town. I told them I didn't believe them and that the dog's owner was looking for him. They didn't argue with me, and they let me take the dog," the officer explained.

"I had almost given up ever seeing my dog again!" Betty exclaimed. "By the way, what two men had the dog?" she asked.

"I didn't ask them their names," the officer said, "I must hurry back to patrolling the streets."

Bingo jumped out of the police car and followed Betty to the van. He was so glad to be back where he belonged. He stretched out on the couch in the back of the van and smiled his biggest smile. He was asleep before Betty left town to go to the farm.

It was cool to have Bingo back. Betty thought Bingo would run around the farm and enjoy his old home, but Bingo was not interested in the old farm anymore. Maybe he was too much of a city dog now. Bingo just lay close to Betty's feet and watched her work.

Betty fell over Bingo once when she had her arms full of junk. "Oh, Bingo, you seem to be a lazy dog now!" she exclaimed.

Betty worked until noon. She shared her lunch and water with Bingo. Betty took a short nap on the only small bed left in the old house. She used Bingo for a pillow.

By the end of the week, milo harvest was over, Betty had the little house as clean as possible, and she and Bingo were ready to go back to the city.

Betty and Bingo ate Thanksgiving dinner at Martin's. Betty's other son, Don, and Betty's parents were also there. Betty enjoyed visiting with the family, and Bingo had a great time playing with Bobby. After dinner, Betty and Bingo kissed everyone good-bye and started the long trip back to the city.

Bingo watched the traffic for awhile before he went to sleep on the sofa in the back. It was almost dark when Betty drove the van back up the mountain, and to their beautiful new home.

Bingo was glad to be home. Joe and Sambo were glad to see Bingo too. It was a happy family that went to bed that night.

. . .

CHAPTER VIII

Back in the City

Bingo was so happy to be home that he stayed in the yard almost as well as if there was a fence around it. Sambo had learned to leave the paper boy alone and was free from the chain again. Bingo didn't see any mean steers around so he was brave enough to bark at people and dogs that came by the yard.

The only time Bingo left the yard was to visit the neighbor across the street. He waited beside the neighbor's car every morning. Every morning when Mr. Walters came out to his car, to go to work, he took time to hug Bingo's neck and tell him good-bye.

For several weeks Bingo told the neighbor good-bye and spent the rest of the day helping Sambo guard the yard by barking

One day Betty was washing the van. She washed the outside and cleaned the inside. Betty thought her work was almost done when she opened the door to finish cleaning the windows. She noticed muddy foot-prints on the carpet leading to the couch in the back. The muddy foot-prints were even on the couch and Bingo was lying in the middle of the couch with his large, muddy feet.

"Oh Bingo, how could you get my clean car dirty?" Betty asked. "I wish you would learn to wipe off your feet before you climb into the van." "Out with you, Bingo!" Betty shouted.

Bingo knew by the sound of Betty's voice that he had done something wrong. He jumped off the couch, out of the van, and crawled under the back porch with his tail tucked between his legs. Betty washed the carpet of the van and went back into the house.

Bingo stayed under the porch a long time. He did not like to make Betty sad. Bingo forgot about Betty when he saw a man leading his dog by the yard. He ran to the edge of yard and helped Sambo bark. The man and his dog quickly walked across the street. Bingo forgot about the property line and ran out of the yard after them.

Bingo did not see another dog standing on the sidewalk. He ran right into it. Both dogs whined as they collided and fell backward. Bingo sat up and looked at the most beautiful dog he had ever seen.

The dog was a black and white collie. She was tall and slender, and her hair was long and shiny. The collie blinked her eyes at Bingo.

Bingo forgot that the rest of the world was around him. He forgot about the man and his dog. Bingo forgot about Sambo. He forgot about Betty and how awful it had been to be away from home and Joe.

The collie ran into Bingo's yard. Bingo ran after her. She ran into the yard next door and Bingo caught up with her again. Bingo ran into the vacant lot across the street and was happy that the beautiful collie followed him. The two dogs had fun chasing each other when suddenly the collie quit chasing Bingo and trotted back across the street.

Bingo barked but the collie would not stop so Bingo ran after her. The collie did not slow down and ran over a hill. They were soon running down a street that Bingo had not seen before.

Bingo whined for the collie to stop. He heard Betty calling him. Bingo looked back. The black and white collie was getting away. Bingo whined as he decided what to do. He ran after the beautiful collie.

Betty was still calling Bingo when the telephone rang. It was Martin. "Mom, we were in the city and thought we would come by and spend the night with you and Joe," Martin said.

"That sounds great. I'll fix some refreshment while you are on your way over," Betty said. She hung up the phone and started the coffee maker. Betty placed some donuts and cookies on the table and waited for Martin, Kasey, and grandson Bobby to arrive. She forgot about Bingo.

The collie did not look at Bingo again, but ran slowly down the mountain through several neighborhoods. The two dogs crossed several streets.

Bingo ran in front of the collie. The collie just ran around him and did not slow down. Bingo followed the collie to a street of smaller houses. The collie ran up a driveway and scratched on the front door. A small child opened the door and the beautiful collie disappeared into the house. The door closed and Bingo was left alone outside. He whimpered and lay down on the front porch and waited for the collie.

Bingo looked around. Nothing looked familiar. He waited and waited, but the collie did not come back outside. The shadows east of the trees grew larger and larger. It was starting to get dark. Bingo knew he needed to go back home but where was home?

Finally Bingo trotted away from the house where the collie had disappeared. He ran down a one-way street looking for something he recognized feeling frightened. He ran down the street until he came to a dead end. Bingo ran across some empty space on the side of the mountain, and between another row of houses. He panicked and ran in a different direction.

Bingo heard a couple of dogs barking at him so he ran in another direction. It was soon too dark to see where he was running.

There was a street light up ahead. Bingo saw a small house with a hedge of trees on one side. It looked like a safe place to spend the night. He would have to try to find his way when it was daylight. Bingo crawled under the hedge and curled up into a furry ball. He tried to keep warm. Bingo was afraid, hungry, thirsty, cold, and very lost.

After sleeping for awhile, Bingo was awakened by a strange noise. The noise almost sounded like the wind was blowing hard. But, the wind was not blowing. Then Bingo saw it. It was the largest cat he had ever seen. In fact, the cat was more than twice as big as Bingo.

The big cat

The cat made the terrible noise again. Bingo backed under the bushes until he was against the yard fence. The large cat was walking toward him roaring. Bingo saw the cat's huge tail twitching while the cat walked quietly closer and closer. Bingo was afraid to even breathe. He did not know it was a huge mountain lion.

Suddenly there was another noise. The huge cat turned in the direction of the noise and made another terrifying noise. Then Bingo saw another animal. It was a black and white cat like he had seen on the farm a long time ago.

Bingo remembered when he smelled his terrible odder. It almost made him sick. He remembered how his mother, Lucky, used to kill these horrible smelling cats.

The black and white cat walked toward the huge cat. It had its tail up. The huge cat shook his head and snorted. It started to back up. The huge cat coughed, turned around, and ran up the mountain.

The black and white cat turned and walked the other way. It walked close to where Bingo was hiding. Bingo needed to cough, but he held his breath until the stinky cat was away from the hedge. Bingo shook his head and coughed. He was no longer hungry. He had to find another place to hide that did not stink.

Running to another street light, Bingo crawled in between a fence and garage to wait until morning. He tried to go to sleep but thought he could hear the huge cat strange noises again. It took him a long time to go to sleep.

Joe and Betty took Bobby to a fun place called the North Pole that afternoon where he visited Santa Clause's workshop and gave Santa some candy. He joined some other children that were sliding down slides that looked like giant candy canes. Joe and Betty watched Bobby ride on a Ferris wheel that looked like a giant Christmas tree. The whole family took a ride on a small train that went all around the North Pole

Joe and Betty took the family out to supper before they came home. They went to a pizza place that had fun games. They were late getting home.

"Where is Bingo?" Joe asked when only Sambo came out to greet them as they drove into the yard.

"I don't know," Betty replied, "I saw him go over that hill over there and he was following a beautiful black and white collie." I hope he isn't lost again."

Bingo blinked his eyes. The sun was shining. Bingo stood up and peeked out from behind the garage. He did not see a huge cat or a black and white cat so he started to run. He ran up and down two streets when he saw a hill that looked familiar. Bingo barked softly and ran toward the hill. He saw another hill and Joe and Betty's house at the top. He ran up the hill and trotted into his own yard.

Sambo met Bingo. Bingo was so happy he wanted to run and play with his dad. Sambo did not want to be bothered so Bingo lay on the porch with Sambo and tried to rest. They watched Joe and Betty help their company put suitcases into their van. Everyone waved good bye and the van drove away from the house and down the mountain.

"There's Bingo. Now we don't have to look for him," Betty said, "Maybe he was here all the time." She sat down between the dogs and petted them.

Joe went inside to use the telephone.

It was awhile before Bingo could go to sleep without thinking about the huge cat that almost ate him. "I hope I never see him again," he thought.

Bingo did the same thing every morning. He would run across the street to tell Mr. Walters good-bye when he left for work, and then he would stand in line with the children waiting for the school bus so the kids could pet him. After the children left on the bus it was time to help Sambo guard the house where Joe and Betty lived. Bingo never saw the beautiful collie again. "I guess she didn't really love me," he said to himself with a whine.

It was too cold for the dogs to sleep outside but they were always anxious to get outside in the morning. The days were still warm.

The dogs had done their "business" and resting on the porch when Bingo remembered it was time for Mr. Walters to go to work. He ran across the street and lay down beside the car that was parked beside Mr. Walters's house. A friend of Mr. Walters was helping him paint his house. Bingo did not know that Mr. Walters was not going to work.

Mr. Mays came out of the house. He patted Bingo on the head and crawled into his car.

"Del, you're wanted on the telephone," Mr. Walters yelled.

Mr. Mays went back into the house to answer the phone. He forgot to close the car door.

Bingo jumped into the back seat of Mr. May's car and waited for a ride.

A few minutes later Mr. Mays came out of the house, crawled into his car, and started to his home on the other side of the mountain top. He pushed a button on the sun visor of the car. Bingo heard a funny noise as the garage door came up. Mr. Mays drove into the garage and pushed the button again and the garage door closed as Bingo heard the noise again.

Mr. Mays crawled out of the car. Before he could close the car door, Bingo jumped out. Mr. Mays was surprised and jumped back. "You're the dog I saw on the other side of the mountain, aren't You?" He asked. Bingo smiled and ran around the garage looking for a way out.

"Don't worry, boy, I'll take you back after I eat lunch," said Mr. Mays.

Bingo followed Mr. Mays into the house.

Del Mays fixed himself a sandwich. He put a bowl of water on the floor for Bingo, and then he fixed a plate of left-over people food for Bingo's lunch.

After they had finished lunch, Bingo followed Del into the family room. Del sat down to rest.

Bingo sat down next to Del's chair.

You are a very pretty dog, and very well trained," Del said, "I feel tired, and I think I'll go upstairs to rest."

Bingo followed Del upstairs to the huge bedroom. When Del lay down, Bingo jumped on the bed next to him like he had jumped upon Charlie's bed.

"You can't jump on the beds around here," Del said, "My wife would be angry if she found dog prints or dog hair on the beds. You are such a lovable dog, I wished you belonged to us. My son, Delly, needs a dog, but I don't know if my wife would agree to us having another dog."

Bingo looked at Mr. Mays and turned his head from side to side trying to figure out what his friend was saying.

"I didn't think I ever wanted another dog when my old dog died, but you have made me change by mind," Del Mays said. "I wonder if you really do belong to someone, but of course you do, or you wouldn't look so healthy." He gave Bingo a hug the gently pushed him off the bed.

Bingo jumped down to the floor and stretched out. He soon heard funny sounds coming from the bed. Bingo put his front paws up on the bed. The sounds were coming from Mr. Mays. Bingo tried to sleep but the sounds kept him awake.

It was an hour before Del Mays woke up. "I need to get back and help my friend paint," Del said. "Come on, boy," he called to Bingo as he went down the stairs.

Bingo was following Mr. Mays out to the garage when Mr. Mays slammed the door in his face. Bingo whined.

"You stay there until I decide what to do with you," Mr. Mays said. He climbed into his car, pushed the button and the garage door opened, and backed the car out of the garage. He started driving across the mountain top.

"What's the matter with you, Del Mays?" he asked himself, "That dog is not yours and you should be taking him back to his side of the mountain."

Del started to turn the car around. "Lord, I'm not well, and I need a dog like that to keep me company," he said to himself. Mr. Mays drove on to his friend's house across the street from Joe and Betty's.

Bingo whined. He scratched on the door going to the garage. Bingo lay down on the rug next to the door to wait. He finally decided that his new friend was not coming back. Bingo ran through the kitchen and back into the family room. He pushed on the sliding glass door where he could see outside. Nothing moved to let Bingo out. He ran to the large living room and pushed on the front door. It did not move. Bingo pushed on the large windows facing the yard. Nothing moved.

Bingo ran up the stairs and tried the sliding glass doors in the bedroom. He could see outside but the doors would not open. Bingo ran through the house trying every door and window in the four bedrooms and two baths upstairs. Nothing would open and let him out of the house.

Bingo ran back down to the family room next to Mr. May's chair. He lay down for a few minutes when he saw another stairway going down. He ran down the stairs and pushed against the sliding glass door in another family room that had a pool table in it. The doors would not move. Bingo jumped up on his hind legs and pushed on every high window downstairs. Everything was locked and Bingo could not get out.

Bingo ran back to the door going to the garage and lay down to wait. "Maybe Betty will come and get me," he thought.

"I'm not feeling well today, and I think I'll go home early and rest," Del Mays said.

"Then that's what you better do," Wade Walters relied. He went into his garage and brought out the washing equipment for the two men's paint brushes. "We only have the west side of the house to do, and we can do that next week," Wade said.

"I'll help you when I'm feeling better," Del said. He was soon on his way to his side of the mountain top. "I need to get home and rest, and decide what to do with that beautiful dog," Del said to himself.

Bingo was glad to see Del. He greeted his new friend with his best smile and dog wag.

Del hugged Bingo's neck. "You are so much fun that I might get well by just having you around," he said, "If I can just figure out a way to keep you."

Del rested in his chair with Bingo lying by his side again.

"Get up boy, it's time for me to go to the school and pick up my son Delly," Del said, "We have to pick him up from football practice. I'm glad the football field is close to the school or I would have to pick him up from school and take him to practice, and then pick him up after practice,"

Bingo turned his head from side to side trying to figure out what Del was saying. He followed his new friend to the kitchen door that went to the garage. Bingo stopped at the door remembering that the door had been shut in his face before.

Come on boy, you can go this time," said Del.

Bingo ran through the door and jumped into the car where Del was holding the door open for him. He was always ready for a ride. Bingo heard the strange noises again as the garage door opened and closed. Bingo wondered where they were going.

Del had driven several minutes when Bingo saw Joe and Betty's house go by. He whined and laid his head on his paws.

"It's all right," Del said, petting Bingo on the head. He drove down the mountain and across part of the city. Bingo saw a large building. Del parked in front of the building. "We're just in time. Here comes Delly now," he said.

"Hi Dad," Delly said. He was tall like his father and probably weighed two-hundred pounds. "I thought I was going to have to wait on you this evening," the young man told his father. Delly started to crawl into to the car when he saw Bingo and stopped. "Where did you find such a pretty dog, Dad," he asked.

"Well, it's a long story," Del answered. "Would you like to keep him if we can work things out with your mother?" he asked.

"Cool!" Delly exclaimed. He hugged Bingo's neck.

"This is the dog I have always wanted," Delly said.

Bingo smiled and gave a tail wag.

"But, mom said no more dogs when your old dog died last year," Delly reminded his father.

"If you want him bad enough, we just might be able to talk her into letting you keep him," Del explained, "We would both have to take care of him and train him because your mother has all the work she can do already."

If your mother gives you permission to keep him, what will you name him?" Del asked.

"He's big and mostly black," Delly said, "I think I'll name him after a cool football player, Franco Harris."

"I think that's a great name, but don't get to loving the dog too much until we are sure we can keep him," Del warned.

"You are as crazy over him as I am, Dad," Delly said with smile.

They returned home and Bingo rested beside Del's chair again. Delly fixed ice tea and put some sweet rolls in the microwave. He gave Bingo some pieces of the sweet roll.

They had not finished their refreshment when they heard Delly's mother driving into the garage. Bingo heard the garage door too, and ran to the door to greet anyone that came in.

"Come back here and sit down!" Del shouted, "We have to impress Harriett on how well trained you are."

Bingo lay back down beside Del's chair until he heard the kitchen door open. He could not sit still any longer. He ran to the door and greeted Harriett with his best smile and tail wag.

Harriett jumped back. "What on earth is this!" she exclaimed.

"It's a dog, Mother," said Delly

"I know it's a dog, but what is it doing in this house?" she shouted.

"What is a dog doing in my house?" Harriett exclaimed!

"Dad found him. Isn't he pretty, Mom?" Delly asked.

"I have to admit that he's as pretty as a dog CAN be, but you can't keep him!" Harriett exclaimed.

"But, Dad and I will take care of him, and he won't be any extra work for you," Delly argued.

"I don't care what you say. We don't need a dog, "Harriett said, "I'm going upstairs and I want the dog gone, when I come back, understand!"

After Harriett had disappeared, Del said, "I have an idea." He picked up the telephone and called Delly's sister that lived in Indiana. Mary answered before the fourth ring.

"Sis, I have found a beautiful dog and Delly wants to keep him, but your Mother says no," Del explained. "Would you please talk to her and try to talk her into changing her mind?" Del asked his daughter.

"Sure, just put her on the line," Mary answered.

Harriett was just coming down the stairs. "Mom, Sis wants to talk to you," Delly said.

Del handed Harriett the telephone.

Harriett talked a little then she listened to what Mary had to say.

"Mom, dad tells me that he has found a beautiful dog and Delly wants to keep it, "Mary said, "I think you should let him have the dog, I had a dog when I was young, and Dad had a dog until a year ago, but Delly has never had a dog of his own."

Harriett listened while she frowned at Del and Delly. "I'll think about it," she said, and hung up the phone. "That's not fair to bring Mary in on this," Harriett said.

Bingo did not know what Harriett was saying, but he did not like the sound of her voice. He walked over to where Harriet was sitting and put one paw on her lap. He smiled at her and tried wagging his tail.

"Franco, sit!" Del shouted.

"That's all right," Harriet said, "He is a pretty dog and well behaved."

Bingo quickly sat down by Del's chair again.

"I guess we can keep him, even though I need to have my head examined to say yes to another dog in the house," Harriett said.

"Thanks!" both Del and Delly said.

"You can thank me if he makes any messes around the house and you two have to clean them up," Harriett replied with a smile and walked over to where Bingo was sitting. She patted him on the head. "Welcome to our family," Harriet said. She walked into the kitchen and started the evening meal.

"Well, that's taken care of," Delly said. "But, how are we going to make him legally ours?" he asked.

"I have decided to call the dog catcher and have him put in the dog pound," Dell said, "If no one claims him within a week, we can pay his fine and he will legally be ours."

"We just hope and pray that it won't happen," Del answered. He picked up the phone and dialed the city dog catcher. "We have a dog in our garage that we would like for you to pick up this evening," Del told the person at the other end of the line. "How soon can you be here to pick him up?" he asked.

"I can leave right away," the dogcatcher said.

Del had to explain to Harriett why he had called the dog catcher to pick up Bingo.

"I don't know if you are doing the right thing or not," Harriett replied, "He might belong to someone that wants to keep him."

"I don't think we could find another dog as pretty and as well trained as this dog, and I don't know how we could find the owner. If the owner is looking for him they will check the animal shelter anyway before the week is over," Del explained.

Del opened the garage door when he heard the dog catcher drive into the driveway. Bingo stayed close to Delly.

"Where did this animal come from?" the dog catcher asked.

"He came into our yard and would not go away," Del said. "Oh, Lord, forgive me for not telling the truth," he thought. "We like him and if no one claims him within a week, we want to pay his fine so he will be ours." Del tried to explain.

"I have five-hundred dogs in the pound right now that need homes, but none of them are as pretty as this one," the dog catcher said, "I have four other dogs, but if you decide that you don't want him by the end of the week, I want him."

"I'm sure we won't change our minds," Delly said petting Bingo. "But, it's nice to know that no matter what happens, Franco won't ever be shot." He gave Bingo another hug and led him to the dog catcher truck.

Bingo was ready to jump in the front of the truck with the nice man, but the man picked him up and put him into the back of the truck. "He sure is heavy," the dog catcher said.

"Bye Franco. We will see you tomorrow," Delly whispered. He waved as the truck drove away from the house.

CHAPTER IX
The Dog Pound.

Bingo looked out through the windows of the dog wagon. The windows had bars across them and there was no way to get out and try to find Betty and Joe. The floor was bare and cold, and the little pickup truck bed stunk like other dogs. Bingo whined and lay down. His stiff body slid back and forth across the wagon as the pickup truck drove around the curves going down the mountain. Bingo was frightened and he did not understand why Del and Delly had been so nice to him, and then put him in this cold, scary place.

The truck drove onto the interstate highway a few miles, and then turned on an exit in the middle of the city. The dog catcher drove up to a long, white building that said, "Animal Humane Society" on the front. He drove around to the back of the building and stopped the truck.

Bingo heard the man unlocking his prison door. He was getting ready to jump and run when the dog catcher quickly put a chain on his collar and pulled him out of the truck. He pulled Bingo to a small door. "I hate to do this to you, old boy, but I have to," he said. The man unfastened the chain and pushed Bingo through a low door.

Bingo tumbled into a large room with a cold cement floor. The room was cold a filled with dogs. Five-hundred dogs begin barking as soon as they saw Bingo. The room was large, and it did not have much light. What Bingo noticed more than the noise was the terrible stink coming from the dogs. It made him sick at his stomach.

The dogs barked and barked.

Little Messy.

Bingo forgot his stomach ache when he saw all the dogs running at him and barking. He ran into the nearest corner to better protect his hind parts, and then he turned to face the huge pack of dogs. Bingo barked. "If the dogs are going to kill me, I'm going to fight to the last," Bingo told himself.

The dogs stopped about two feet away. They did not come any closer.

Bingo stopped barking and started to growl.

The other dogs were not afraid but they turned around and walked in a different direction. Some of the dogs lay down to sleep while others barked. The barking went on all night.

Bingo grew so tired he finally lay down and tried to go to sleep. He was afraid, lonely, hungry, and thirsty. "Where are Joe and Betty, and why don't they come and get me?" Bingo wondered. He had only napped a little before the sun began to shine. The lights went off in the large room and there were rays of sunshine coming through a row of windows. The dogs continued barking until the dog catcher came through the door. Bingo soon found out why the dogs stopped barking.

The dog catcher and blonde lady came into a screened off section of the room. The dog catcher poured dog food into the trays between the screen and the large room. The lady pulled a water hose to the other trays between the dog food trays and filled them with water. The dogs were too busy drinking and eating to pay any attention to Bingo for awhile.

Bingo was still against the wall. He slowly, and carefully, scooted his body across the one wall until he reached one of the water trays. Bingo took a long drink, but he did not feel like trying any of the dog food because the room stunk so badly.

Bingo saw low doors going outside. "Now was his chance to get away. He took his turn to go through one of the low doors and made a fast run outside. Bingo ran into a fence and bounced back. He walked the length of the fence, but there was no way to escape. Bingo took his turn to go back through the gate. He slowly, and carefully, scooted back into his corner.

The dogs ignored Bingo after they finished eating and drinking. Bingo was ready to get some sleep while the room wasn't so noisy. He was asleep when he thought he heard something. He was frightened and opened his eyes. He was not in danger. A little dog that was part poodle and part Chihuahua was snuggling up against him.

The dog may have been pretty at one time, but now she looked terrible. Her hair was long and tangled. She was skinny and dirty. Bingo turned his head the other way because the little dog stunk terrible.

Messy lay down close to Bingo and whined. Bingo felt sorry for her. Two larger dogs growled for Messy to move away from Bingo, but Messy would not move. The other dogs finally walked away and left them alone.

Messy was a true friend.

Messy felt safe close to Bingo. She followed him to the drinking pan and they drank together. Other dogs growled and tried to bite Bingo, but Messy stood between Bingo and the other dogs. Bingo did not feel so lonely with Messy next to him. He gradually became used to her awful odor.

The next morning the dog catcher came in with another man dressed in white. The two men were wearing heavy gloves. They grabbed the collars of several dogs and checked the numbers that were tied to the collars. Some of the dogs had the right numbers and were pulled out of the room. The dogs never came back.

Messy snuggled up to Bingo and shook. Bingo felt frightened too.

Later in the morning the dog catcher returned and used the water hose to wash out the large room. He sprayed the water over the cement floor until the dog messes were washed into a drain next to the back wall. That afternoon, Del and Delly came to visit.

"Hello, Franco," Delly said.

The name sounded strange, but Bingo ran to the fence to greet them. He smiled his best smile and wagged his tail. "Now I can get out of this place," Bingo told himself.

Just six more days and we can get you out of here," Del said.

Just be a good dog, and then you can go home with us," said Delly.

Bingo turned his head from side to side, trying to figure out what the two men were saying.

"Good-dye, see you tomorrow," Delly and Del said and walked away.

Bingo watched Del and Delly walk away. He sat down next to the fence and cried. Messy sit down beside him and cried too.

Bingo was feeling weak and ate a little dog food the second day. He and Messy drink together and ate together. Bingo did not notice the terrible stink so much now, and he knew that his own fur was dirty and stinky too.

That afternoon Bingo heard Delly calling him. He ran back outside into the fenced area to see his friends. Bingo smiled his best smile, and wagged his best wag. He stood up tall and tried to look pretty. "This is the day they are going to get me out of here," Bingo thought.

Del and Delly talked to Bingo and they walked away again. Bingo lay down and cried again. He heard Messy crying next to him. The two dogs went back inside and walked back to their corner. Bingo lay down to cry and Messy lay down and cried beside him.

Every day the dog catcher and the lady came in a fed and watered the dogs. Ever afternoon the dog catcher washed out the large room. The dog catcher would come back with the man dressed in white and check the numbers on the dog collars. Every day the two men took some of the dogs out of the room. None of the dogs ever came back, but there were new dogs put in every day. The other dogs barked at the new dogs like they did Bingo when he first came into the room.

Bingo noticed that he was the only dog that did not have a number fastened to his collar. The two men never checked him.

"I guess no one wants me, and I'll never get out of this terrible place," Bingo thought.

Messy whined.

That afternoon a lady and her little girl came to the fence. All the dogs ran to the fence and barked. I want that dog, mommy," the little girl said. She pointed to Bingo.

Bingo smiled his best smile.

"He is a pretty dog," the mother said, "Let's talk to the dog catcher and tell him we want that dog."

"That is the only dog that you can't have," the dog catcher tried to explain.

The little girl started to cry.

"Then why do you have that dog in with the others?" the mother asked.

"Because someone has already asked for him, mam," the dog catcher said.

The little girl cried louder.

"That's not fair; see what you have done to my child!" the mother yelled.

"Lady, there are a lot of dogs out there that need homes. Can't you choose another dog, please," the dog catcher asked.

Delilah stopped crying. "If I can't have that dog, I don't want any dog!" she shouted and started crying again.

"I still think this is unfair!" The mother was still shouting, "Come on dear," she said pulling the crying child away from the building.

"I guess I'm not pretty enough to get out of here," Bingo was thinking. He heard Delly calling him and went to the fence and tried to look impressive. The two men talked to him and then walked away. Bingo went back to his corner and cried. Messy lay down beside him and cried too.

The third day there was feeding, watering, and cleaning of pens. The two men came in and took more dogs. One man picked up Messy. Messy whined and looked at Bingo. Bingo did not know what to do. The man checked Messy's number and put her back down. Messy snuggled up to Bingo and whined again. Bingo felt her skinny body shaking against him.

That afternoon there were more visitors. A young boy asked for Bingo and was told that he had already been asked for. "Gee Whiz,that is the only pretty dog you have here!" he exclaimed before he walked away.

On the fourth day the dogs were fed and watered. The man in white came back with the dog catcher and they checked the numbers of the dog tags again. The man in white checked Messy's number. "Sorry, old girl, your time is up," he said. The man picked up Messy. Messy whined as the man was taking her out of the room. She looked at Bingo and whined. Bingo whined but he didn't know what to do.

Other dogs were taken out of the large room. None of them ever came back.

Bingo waited and waited for Messy to come back, but somehow he knew that she would never come back. Now Bingo was more lonesome than ever. "Maybe I should have fought the man in white," he told himself, "It's too late now, and maybe Messy is in a better place than this, now," Bingo thought.

There were more visitors, but they only chose the best dogs to take out of the room. "Why doesn't anyone pick me?" Bingo wondered.

Del and Delly came by to see Bingo. Bingo was lying outside in the sunshine trying to get warm.

"Come here Franco," Delly called. Bingo tried to smile, but he was too sad to walk over to the fence to see the two men he thought had been his friends.

Just three more days, and you will be ours," Delly said, "Just be brave, Franco and we will get you out of this place."

Bingo laid his head on his paws. He did not know what Delly was saying. "I'll never get out of this horrible place," he was thinking. He knew he was dirty, smelly, and could no longer hold his head high and look proud. Betty, Joe, and Messy were the only ones that really loved me, and they are all gone now," Bingo thought.

The fifth and sixth day Bingo went inside when he saw Del and Delly coming to visit. Delly called and called but Bingo backed into his corner in the big room. He was not going to get excited and then be disappointed anymore.

"Joe, I don't think Bingo is on the mountain," Betty said, "I've driven all over this area and I can't find him anywhere. I think we should check at that animal shelter I saw from the interstate highway the other day."

"There is no way Bingo could end up in that place," Joe replied, "I think you are right that someone has stolen him again. You were right the first time when you said that Bingo had been dog-napped, and it wouldn't do any good to check the animal shelter. But, if we don't find him by this weekend, we will take a chance and look there on Saturday.

"Joe, what happens to dogs that the shelter can't give away?" Betty asked.

"I think they keep them so long and then shoot them," Joe answered.

"Oh how awful!" Betty exclaimed, "I'm glad that Bingo is too pretty for that to happen to him."

. . .

CHAPTER X
Who Will Get Bingo?

On the sixth day, Del was talking to Mr. Walters on the phone. "We're getting a dog tomorrow," Del said.

"That's nice," Mr. Walters replied. What kind of puppy are you getting," he asked.

"He is a beautiful dog, friendly, mostly black, but he has white feet, and thick fur," Del answered.

"You mean that you are getting a full-grown dog?" Mr. Walters asked, "I thought you were just buying a puppy from someone."

"I think he is almost grown," Del said.

"Where did you find him?" Mr. Walters asked.

"We are getting him from the animal shelter, or what some people call the dog pound," Del answered.

"I thought you would buy a registered dog." Mr. Walters said and hung up. He thought for a minute and called Del back. "Del, that sounds like my neighbor's dog," Mr. Walters said, "He has been missing for several days. Do you remember that you petted him beside your car that day?"

"But we want the dog!" Del exclaimed.

"If you don't tell them about the dog, I will!" Mr. Walters exclaimed.

"But what if it is their dog and they want to give him away, or even sell him?" Del asked. "Besides, if they really care about the dog, they would have been looking for him already."

"They might give him away because they have had a hard time keeping him in their yard," Mr. Walters said, "They have another large dog and they don't have a fence to keep in their dogs. All you can do is talk to them and ask them. If you don't tell them, then I will."

"All right, I will go talk to them," Del replied.

It was cold as Del climbed up the steps to the large green-colored house where Joe and Betty lived. He did not feel well, and he felt shaky. His hand shook as he rung the doorbell.

Betty answered the door. She was surprised to see a tall, thin, sickly-looking, white-haired man standing on the step. He looked cold, so Betty took a chance and invited him inside.

Betty was surprised to see a sickly-looking man at the door!

"May I please have your dog?" the man asked.

"H-H-Have you p-p-people lost a d-d-dog?" Del managed to ask. He hadn't stuttered for a long time.

"Yes we have?" Betty exclaimed. "Have you found our Bingo?" she asked.

"Y-Y-Yes Mam, I-I-I think we m-m-might have," Del answered. "H-H-He came into our y-y-yard and w-w-we couldn't get rid of h-h-him, so I c-c-called the dog p-p-pound,"

"Oh great!" Betty exclaimed, "Now we can go get him."

"M-M-Mam, would you p-p-please give us your d-d-dog?" Del asked, "I-I-I'm not well and I n-n-need a dog for c-c-company in the d-d-day time."

Betty started to say no but the man kept talking.

I h-h-have a son t-t-that loves the d-d-dog," Del stuttered, "W-W-We have even called my d-d-daughter in I-I-Illinois to talk her m-m-mother into I-I-letting us have the d-d-dog, and w-w-we have b-b-bought dog f-f-food, c-c-collars, d-d-dishes, and t-t-toys for the d-d-dog. My son h-h-has even named him F-F-Franco

Harris after h-h-his favorite f-f-football player," Del said without giving Betty a chance to say anything.

"No, we won't give Bingo away, because we love him too!" Betty shouted, "There are many dogs in this city that need homes!" "Why do you have to want our dog?" she asked.

"W-W-We will build a f-f-fence around our b-b-back yard so h-h-he will never g-g-get run over or r-r-run away," Del said.

"We don't own this house, and we can't build a fence for Bingo," Betty told herself. "Joe, come in here!" Betty yelled.

Joe did not come into the room. Betty called Joe again. There was no sound in the family room where Joe had been sitting. "Please sit down right there while I find my husband," Betty said, pointing to a large chair in the living room. Betty walked through the family room, dining room, and down the long hall to the master bedroom. Joe was standing behind the bedroom door in the dark.

"I don't know what to do about Bingo," Joe said.

"It is sad to give Bingo away," Betty said.

"Joe, there is a man in our living room that is asking for Bingo," Betty said.

"I know. I heard what he said," Joe replied.

"Then why didn't you come when I called you?" Betty asked.

"Because I don't know what to do," Joe answered. Then Joe stomped his feet and said, "Yes I do know what to do!" He walked out to where Del Mays was sitting.

Del saw Joe coming and stood up. "W-W-We want your d-d-d-g and I'll be glad to p-p-pay you any price you say," Del said before Joe had a chance to say anything, "M-M-My son n-n-needs him, and I . . ."

Joe would not let Del finish what he was trying to say. "I heard your story!" Joe shouted. "We love our dog and we will not sell him? We can't build a fence to keep him, and I might have considered giving him to you but you lied to us. I don't want to give Bingo to a man who lies! I know you stole him and kept him penned up so he couldn't come back home! We know he didn't come around your place and would not leave!"

"I'm sorry I-I-I lied, but h-h-he jumped into my c-c-car and I took him h-h-home with me and I d-d-didn't know h-h-he was in my c-c-car," Del stuttered.

"I can believe that," Joe and Betty both said.

"What happened next?" Joe asked.

"I was p-p-planning on b-b-bringing him b-b-back to t-t-this n-n-neighborhood and then I d-d-decided to try and k-k-keep him," Dell answered.

"Didn't you know he belonged to someone?" Joe asked, still angry.

"Yes, b-b-but I thought w-w-we needed him m-m-more than the owner d-d-did," Del answered. "I knew t-t-the only way he c-c-could be l-l-legally ours was t-t-to call the d-d-dog pound, hope n-n-no one claimed h-h-him, p-p-pay his fine, and t-t-take him home. I-I-I'm not well. I-I-I'll pay you. I-I-I'll build a fence for h-h-him."

"I guess I'll give Bingo to you, only because we can't build a fence for him," Joe said, "Now get out of here before I change my mind!"

"Thank you," Del said. He opened the front door, and then he turned around. "Y-Y-You can come to visit h-h-him any time you w-w-want to. W-W-We live on 2695 Pine R-R-Road."

"Thanks," Betty replied with sobs.

Joe had left the room. Betty looked through the window facing the street. She watched Del descend the steps and walk across the street to his car. Betty had tears rolling down her face. She went to find Joe. Joe was back in the dark bedroom. He didn't say anything, but Betty thought Joe was crying too.

The next morning Joe said, "Don't fix breakfast yet. I want to drive to the address that Mr. Mays gave us last night see if he was telling the truth."

Betty and Joe dressed and put on their heavy coats. They drove to the other side of the mountain top and found the address.

"Oh Joe, look at that!" Betty exclaimed, pointing to a new, large home. "It's beautiful!"

"But we don't know if this where Mr. Mays lives or not," Joe replied.

"I'm sure it is, because I see the car he was driving last night in front of the three-car garage." Betty said,

"Why would people this rich want our Bingo instead of buying an expensive, registered dog?"

"I think you can answer that question," Joe said. They did not talk for the next several days.

On the seventh day, Bingo was so sad and lonely that he went up to the man in white and asked (in dog language) for the man to take him.

"If the owners don't want this dog today, can I take him?" the man in white asked.

"I'm sure they will claim him today," the dog catcher answered. "They have been here every day to visit him, besides if they don't come for him I have already asked for him.

"You sure are popular, old boy, but I can't take you with me," the man in white said. He patted Bingo on the head.

Bingo walked away. "No one wants me," he thought. Bingo was so sad that he stayed in his corner all day. He did not lye in the sun to get warm. Bingo did not care if he was cold. He laid his head on his paws and whined.

CHAPTER XI
Freedom

Bingo heard a familiar voice. It was Delly calling him, but Delly was not outside the fence. Delly was standing in the door of the large room.

The dog catcher came in and put a short chain on Bingo's collar and led him to the door. He gave the chain to Delly. Bingo saw Del standing in the next room.

Delly took the chain and patted Bingo on the head. "Sir, may we clean him up in this room before we take him home?" Delly asked.

"Sure," the dog catcher said, "There is a hose in that corner, but I don't have any dog shampoo."

"We have everything we need in the car," Delly explained.

"Go get everything you need and that will give me time enough to give the dog all his shots I need to give him before he leaves here," the man said.

The dog catcher took Bingo's chain and led him into a small room. He lifted Bingo up and put him on a hard table.

Bingo was sad because Delly and Del had left him again. He did not care what happened. Bingo put his head on his paws and whined. He jumped when the dog catcher stuck him with something that felt like a bee sting. "What did he do that for?" Bingo wondered. Bingo felt the bee sting again. "I'm getting out of here," Bingo thought and started to run.

The dog catcher grabbed Bingo's chain and walked him back into the other room. Del and Delly were back.

"I'll take him now," Delly said. He pulled Bingo into a corner of the room and Bingo felt water running through his fur. The water was cold, but it felt good. The shampoo smelled great. Delly was soon drying Bingo with a soft towel. Bingo knew he did not stink anymore. He felt cool and held his head high. Delly finished drying Bingo's hair and gave him a big hug.

Bingo could not believe that he had been so sad just a few minutes ago and now he felt so happy.

Delly put a green sparkly collar around his neck. He threw his old collar into the trash can. Delly put a green leash on Bingo's new collar. "You look like a show dog again, Franco," Delly said and gave Bingo another hug.

"He sure does?" Del exclaimed.

Bingo held his head high and marched out of the terrible building.

"I was hoping you wouldn't come in today," the dog catcher said, "But I knew you would."

The dogs started barking as Bingo marched past the long fence. He stopped and looked inside at the unhappy dogs. "They are not mean, but just afraid," Bingo thought. "I wish I could take all of you with me," he said in dog language. Bingo barked farewell to the dogs barking at him. It seemed like he had been there a long, long time.

It felt so good to be clean again!

CHAPTER XII
A New Home

Bingo rode back up the mountain sitting in the front seat between Del and Delly. He whined when he saw Joe and Betty's house. He wondered if he would ever see his old friends and Sambo again.

Del pushed the button and the garage door opened. Bingo was used to the sound by now.

Delly ran into the house and quickly changed clothes. Del and Bingo stayed in the car. Delly climbed back into the car and Del drove him to school. "I hope you haven't missed too much school this morning," Del said.

Bingo watched Delly disappear into a large building. He watched the cars go by on the busy city streets as Del drove across the city. He felt so free.

Del parked the car in a large parking lot. "You'll have to stay here, Franco, because I can't take you into the grocery store," Del said.

Bingo watched Del walk into a large building. He decided to take a nap. He was dreaming he was back in the terrible room with all the other dogs when he heard children talking. Bingo opened his eyes. There were two small boys looking at him through the car window.

"Mom, I want a dog like that," one boy said.

"I wish we could have a dog like that, but he belongs to someone else, the mother said, "Besides we wouldn't have room for him in our small apartment, and a dog like that needs a yard to play in. Now come along with me because we have to hurry."

Bingo was almost asleep again when Del unlocked the car door and put some sacks in the back seat. "I'm sorry I was gone so long," he said.

Bingo watched the traffic through the city. He looked at the mountains as Del drove up their mountain. He did not whine when he saw Joe and Betty's house this time. He was just glad to be out of the terrible room with all the dogs.

Del turned Bingo loose in the back yard for him to do his business. He followed Del into the house and shared some cookies with him. Bingo took a drink of water from his special dish and followed Del up the stairs. He lay beside Del's bed and heard the funny noises again. Bingo felt clean, loved, and pretty and it was easy for him to go to sleep too.

"Come on Franco," Del said, "We have to pick Delly up early because he has a football game tonight and won't be going to practice."

Bingo leaned his head from side to side, and followed Del back to the car. It did not take them long to arrive at the school. Bingo watched Delly come out of the large building.

"I missed you this afternoon, Franco," Delly said and hugged Bingo's neck. Bingo felt so proud riding home between Del and Delly.

Harriett came home early. She patted Bingo on the head and started the evening meal.

Bingo rested beside Del's chair while Delly did his homework. Bingo ate from his new dish next to the table while the family ate. Delly handed Bingo a piece of meat.

"Don't feed him from the table because it will give him bad manners!" Harriet exclaimed.

Bingo started to jump into the front seat of the car when Delly said, "No, Franco, you have to ride in the back with me when Mom is with us."

Bingo jumped into the back seat and watched the traffic back to the city. Del parked the car next to the largest lawn Bingo had ever seen. Delly jumped out of the car and ran into a large building. He soon came out wearing a bright suit. He put a helmet on his head and ran out to the large grass with the other boys.

Bingo laid his head down to rest when everyone started yelling. "What have I done now to get into trouble?" Bingo thought, jumping up.

The people were honking their car horns, but no one was looking at him. Everyone was watching the boys run back and forth across the grass.

Bingo watched for awhile and then he took a nap. It had been a long day and he didn't know anything about football.

Bingo woke up when the noise stopped. There were two people standing beside the car talking to Del and Harriett.

"What a pretty dog," the man said.

"Yes, we just got him," Del replied. "Delly has never had a dog before we found this one."

Bingo sat up proud.

The Yelling started again. Bingo saw all the boys running back onto the grass. "It would be fun to run on grass like that," Bingo thought. The noise put him to sleep again. The noise finally stopped and Bingo woke up. He listened to Del and Harriett talking in the front seat.

"I missed you during the game, Franco," Delly said when he climbed into the car. He crawled into the back seat and hugged Bingo's neck again.

"That was a great game. Congratulations, son," Del said.

"Yes, we are proud of you," Harriett agreed.

"Thanks," Delly replied. "Was Franco a good dog while I was gone?"

We hardly knew he was back there," Harriett said with a smile, "I guess I'm glad that he is a part of our family now."

They were soon home. When it was time to go to bed Bingo started to lye down beside Del's bed. "I guess you are Delly's dog now so you need to sleep in his room," Del said.

"Here Franco," Delly called.

Bingo ran to Delly's room and jumped on his bed. "No, Franco, you can't sleep on the bed?" Delly exclaimed, pointing to the floor.

Bingo jumped down and lay close to Delly's bed. The house was quiet and everyone was soon asleep. Bingo was thankful that he was not in the terrible place and he tried not to think about Messy and the other dogs.

The next morning Del went to call Delly to get up and get ready for school. He shut Delly's door quickly.

"What's the matter?" Harriett asked, opening the door. "Oh, no," she said, and then she begin to laugh.

Bingo was sleeping on the bed with Delly. Delly had his arms around the huge dog.

"Don't you think he is too old for that?" Harriett said with a chuckle. "I think both of them need some training." She was laughing as she went down stairs to start breakfast.

Bingo and Del took Delly to school. When they came back, he needed to rest in his chair and Bingo was resting beside the chair. "I feel better since I have you to talk to," Del said petting Bingo. The door bell rang. Bingo jumped up and went to the door. "No, Bingo. Sit," Del said.

Bingo came back and sat down beside Del's chair. The door bell rang again but Bingo stayed next to the chair until Del said he could come to the door.

"I'm from the building company, and I'm here to build your fence," the man said.

"Good. Follow me and I'll show you where I want the fence built," Del said. Bingo and the carpenter followed Del to the back yard. "This is our property line," Del said. "I want the fence six feet high and ending here." He explained. "I also want a gate right here," he said pointing close to the side of the house.

"I understand," the man said. "I'll get the post holes dug this morning and the cement truck will be here this afternoon to pour concrete around the post holes," the carpenter explained. "I want the concrete to harden so I won't get any more done than that this week."

"I understand," Del replied, "I'll be glad when the job is done so my dog can run free in the back yard."

"I would not want to tie up a pretty dog like that either," the carpenter said. "Where can I park my truck and unload the lumber?" he asked.

Del showed the man where to unload. "I would help you, but I'm not well," he said.

"Don't worry. I'll do all the work. That's what you are paying me for," the man said with a grin.

Del and Bingo went back into the house to rest.

The carpenter worked several days. Soon Bingo was running across the large yard with the safety of the fence. He ran up the back steps and lay down on the deck outside the bedroom section of the house. He missed Sambo, Joe, and Betty.

The sun felt so warm that the deck became Bingo's favorite place to rest when he was outside. He loved laying on the high platform and looking at the city below him. He liked looking at the beautiful mountains to the west.

One afternoon Bingo was on the deck when he heard Del calling to him. He looked down and saw Betty. Bingo ran down the steps and greeted his old friend.

"Bingo, you look so pretty, and my, how you have grown," Betty said as she hugged Bingo's neck. "I'm sorry but Joe could not come and visit you. I guess he just misses you too much and Sambo misses you too."

Betty sat down to visit with Del while she watched Bingo scamper around his new play area. Bingo came back and lay next to Del's chair. "I can see that you have trained him well, and he doesn't jump up on people now," Betty said. "I must go home, but I'll be back again." She started toward the door. Bingo started to follow her.

"No, Bingo, you must stay here with your new owners now," Betty said hugging Bingo good-bye.

Bingo whined so Del took him to the kitchen for a treat.

The next time Del went to the grocery store he bought Bingo something hard to chew on. It tasted like meat. After Bingo had eaten most of the treat, Del took a bright colored ball from a sack and rolled it in front of Bingo to chase the ball but he was not allowed to run in the house so he stayed sitting beside Del' chair.

"Get the ball, Franco," Del said.

Bingo did not move. Del rolled the ball again. "Get the ball," Del said.

Bingo thought he would take a chance and chase the ball. He looked up and waited for Del to yell at him.

"Go!" Del said.

Bingo ran after the ball. He picked it up and laid it beside Del's chair. "Good dog," Del said. Soon Bingo could catch the ball before it hit the floor when Del threw it.

The days went by quickly. Del and Bingo took Delly to school every morning and picked him up after school every afternoon. On the weekends they could sleep later and play games in the back yard.

Harriett went to work most days and it seemed that she hugged Bingo's neck almost as often as Delly did.

Another Thanksgiving passed with plenty to eat. Bingo enjoyed playing with Delly during that week, but Bingo enjoyed playing with Del when Delly was in school. Del seemed to not need as much rest. Football was soon over and Delly started wrestling. Bingo did not get to go to the wresting matches but he waited in the family car.

Betty came to visit and brought Bingo some doggie treats for Christmas.

He received almost as many gifts as the rest of the family.

Sis came home from Illinois. It was the first time she had seen Bingo. "I think you made a wise choice, Mom" she told Harriett.

. . .

CHAPTER XIII
The Third Dog-Napping

"Del, I need for you to go to the grocery store for me today and buy something special for me to cook for Ground Hog's Day," Harriett said.

"What do you want?" Del asked.

"What else but ground hog," Harriett said with a laugh. "We call it sausage and I need some cinnamon for the apple pies."

Del and Bingo took Delly to school and stopped by the grocery store on their way home.

"I'll hurry so you won't have to wait so long on me this time," Del told Bingo. He hurried into the large store to buy what Harriett wanted. Del forgot to lock the car doors.

Bingo stretched out across the front seat of the car and took a nap. He woke up when he heard footsteps coming to the car. Bingo stood up and smiled, but the person was not Del.

"What a pretty dog," the young man said. "It would be nice to have a dog like that to keep me company." "Why not?" he asked himself. The man turned around and started back toward Del's car. "I'm sure the car is locked," the man said and walked toward his own vehicle and then he stopped and looked around the large parking lot. There was not another person in sight. "Why not check and see. I deserve a nice dog like that," he said.

The man walked over to where Bingo was watching him through the car window. He looked around again, and then he tried to open the door. "This is my lucky day!" the man exclaimed as the door came open. He carefully stuck his hand in and reached for Bingo's collar. "Nice doggie," the man said.

Bingo did not move, growl, or bark.

"Oh good, you're friendly," the man said, "But how am I going to get you to my car? You're too big to carry." He opened the glove compartment and said, "This is really my lucky day," when he saw Bingo's leash. The man quickly put the leash on Bingo collar and gently pulled him toward the door. "Come on boy," he said softly.

Bingo jumped out of the car and looked for Del.

The man patted Bingo and said, "This way, boy," Bingo followed the man to his old pickup truck. "Jump in boy," the man said.

The man sounded so excited that Bingo jumped into the pickup truck and waited for a ride. "Maybe this man is going to take me to Del or Delly," Bingo thought.

The young man looked over the parking lot again and quickly drove away. Bingo watched the traffic go by.

Hank drove to a poor part of the city. He parked his truck in front of a large old building. Hank looked in every direction, grabbed Bingo leash and quickly pulled him up a flight of steps. He unlocked a door and pushed Bingo through it. "We are not supposed to have animals in these apartments so no one can see you,"

Hank closed the door and took the leash from Bingo's collar. Bingo ran to every corner of the apartment looking for a way to escape. The apartment was only one large room and a small bath. The larger room had an unmade bed in one corner, an old couch and chair in another corner, and a few cabinets and sink with two chairs at a table. It was almost dark because all the window shades were closed.

There was only one door, the one they had just come through, and one window. The bath was dark with no windows. Bingo soon found that there was no way to get away. He lay next to the door and whined.

"you dumb dog, I told you to shut up!" the man shouted.

"Shut up you dumb dog?" Hank shouted. Bingo was frightened and whined again. Hank came over and kicked him in the side. "I said for you to shut up!" he shouted in a whisper.

Bingo whined again and Hank kicked him again. Bingo yelped and the man kicked him again. Bingo was hurting but he laid his head on his paws and did not make any more noise.

"I'm sorry dog, but if the owners found you here, they would kick me out," Hank said. He patted Bingo on the head. Hank sat down in the old chair next to the couch.

Bingo knew he could not get away. He knew he was in danger if he did not please the man, so he sat up straight beside the man's chair. "You're well trained. Good dog," Hank said.

Bingo lay down and waited. There was suddenly a terrible odor in the room. It did not smell like a bunch of stinky dogs. It did not smell like the black and white cat, but it was awful. Bingo raised his head. The odor was coming from the man and something on the table. Bingo saw smoke. It made him want to cough, but he held his breathe. He was afraid to cough in case Hank kicked him again.

Bingo laid his head back down. He was frightened, lonely, hungry, thirsty, and his side hurt where the man had kicked him.

"I'm . . . going . . . to . . . take . . . a . . . nap," Hank said and fell across the bed.

Bingo lay down beside the bed on the dirty carpet. He heard Hank coughing, but the man lay still for a long time. When he finally sat up, he said, "I'm hungry. I guess I need to get us something to eat. I'll be back in a little while, dog."

When Hank opened the door, Bingo tried to run through the door but the man kicked him again. "I told you no one can see you around here!" he said and kicked Bingo toward the bed.

Bingo shrunk back against the bed, but he did not cry again. He knew he would just be kicked again. Bingo watched Hank go through the door and heard him lock the door. He heard him go down the steps. Bingo lay down beside the door. It was more fun to be alone than to be with this man.

Bingo was hurting. "Maybe my side won't hurt so much if I lay on the bed," he thought. It didn't help but he laid there until Hank came back. He listened while Hank came up the stairs and unlocked the door. Bingo did not move or try to escape this time.

"I'm glad you're learning to mind," Hank said," I don't like to kick you," He patted Bingo on the head. The man was carrying a brown paper sack. He took out a sandwich and Coke.

Hank filled a cup full of water and put it on the floor and took the bread off his sandwich and gave it to Bingo.

Bingo jumped off the bed and drank all the water. The man filled the cup again and Bingo drank all the water again. He ate all the bread, but he was still hungry. Bingo saw the man put a newspaper on the small table. He remembered how mad Joe and Betty were when he tore up newspapers.

"I guess I'll check the job section to see if I can find a job," Hank said, "It's going to take more money to feed both of us."

Bingo waited.

"@#$!%$^#$" Hank said. "There just isn't any @#$%#^$ jobs in this town!

Bingo lye down beside the chair and put his head down on the paws. The man sounded angry. Was he going to be kicked again? Bingo smelled the terrible odder again. He waited for the man to fall on the bed.

Hank got up from his chair and fell across the bed. Bingo waited. The room grew dark as the sun was setting outside. It was dark when the man woke up. Bingo was excited when Hank put his leash back on his collar. "Maybe he is going to take me home," he thought.

Hank led Bingo down the steps and walked him around some old buildings for him to do his business. When he started back up the stairs, Bingo tried to pull back. He did not want to go back into that dark, dirty place.

Hank jerked Bingo's collar so hard that Bingo thought he was going to stop breathing. He jerked Bingo all the way up the steps and pushed him back through the door. "You better be good or you will never get out of this room!" Hank shouted as he closed the door. "I'm leaving and you better not make any noise," he said and went back out the door.

Bingo listened as the man locked the door and went back down the steps. He went to the cup for another drink but there wasn't any water left. Bingo whined from the pain in his side and because he was thirsty. He jumped back on the bed and went to sleep feeling safe for awhile.

It was a long time before Bingo heard Hank come up the steps, unlock the door, come into the room, and lock the door again. He watched the man fall on the bed again. The terrible odor made him lay next to the door to rest. It seemed like a little air was coming into the room under the door.

Del bought the groceries that Harriett needed. He felt better than he had felt for a long time and he had not gone to the doctor for quite awhile. Del felt happy when he walked up to the SUV. He did not see Bingo. Del hurried to the car and looked into the back seat. It was empty. He tried opening the door.

"Oh! No!" Del exclaimed when he found the car door unlocked. Del put his sacks in the back seat. He ran all over the parking lot calling for Bingo. Del looked down all the streets close to the parking lot.

"I can't believe I forgot to lock the doors!" Del exclaimed, "Franco is too friendly and he has been stolen." "I wonder if Betty and Joe felt this sad when we took Franco?" Del asked himself. He climbed into the car and hurried to the police station.

"I want to report that my dog has been stolen," Del told the dispatcher sitting behind a large desk.

"How do you know your dog has been stolen?" the lady asked, "How do you know it hasn't just run away?"

"Because he was taken from my vehicle," Del replied. "I forgot to lock the car when I went into the store."

"It sounds like he has been stolen," the lady said. "How long has he been missing?" she asked.

"It has been two hours since I left him in the car," Del answered.

"Give me a description of your dog and we'll have our people watch for him," the lady said.

"I don't have to do that because I have a picture of him right here in my wallet," Del replied. He showed the lady Bingo's picture. "The dogs name is Franco, and he weighs about seventy pounds." Del explained.

"He's a very pretty dog, but it's doubtful that the people that took him will return him," the lady said, "They may be a long way from here by now, and they probably won't let anyone see him for awhile, even if they are still in town."

"I'm willing to pay a reward," Del said.

"That might help, but you need to take your reward idea to the local newspaper office and run it in the next paper," the lady said, "I'll make a copy of the dog's picture and put it on our bulletin board so all our officers can look for him."

As soon as the copy was made, Del hurried to the newspaper office. "My dog has been stolen and I want to offer a reward to get him back," Del said, "I want to put an ad in the paper with my dog's picture."

The man turned around and started typing on his computer. "What do you want your ad to say?" he asked.

"One-thousand dollar reward for the return of our dog, Franco, right under his picture," Del replied.

"Do you want your telephone number on the ad," the man asked.

"Yes, and you might mention that Franco weighs seventy pounds," Del said.

After the man finished typing, Del handed him Bingo's picture.

"Nice looking dog," the man said, "We'll see what we can do for you, but it's too late for the ad to be in today's paper." "Will tomorrow do?" he asked.

"I guess it will have to do," Del answered, "I want the ad on the front page."

"That will cost more," the man replied.

"We will spare no expense to get our dog back," Del said. He wrote the man a large enough check to run the ad for a week. Del hurried home with Harriett's groceries. He felt terrible when he had to pick up Delly without Bingo.

"Where's Franco?" Delly asked immediately.

"I forgot to lock the car doors when I went into the grocery store this morning," Del said, "When I cam back, Franco was gone. I'm sorry son."

"Don't worry dad, We'll get our dog back," Delly said.

"I sure hope we can find him, but don't blame yourself, Dad, it could have happened to anyone," Delly said. "You don't look like you feel very well."

"I've put an ad in the newspaper with a reward, so maybe somehow we'll get Franco back," Del said.

"Sure we will, Dad," Delly agreed.

The house was too quiet without Bingo. "I didn't know I would miss that dog so much," Harriett said to herself, "I sure hope someone finds him." She set the meal on the table and called Del and Delly to come to eat.

"Mom, Dad, let's pray that we'll get Franco back," Delly said.

The Mays held hands and Delly prayed that Bingo would be found.

"That's what I should have done as soon as I found out Franco was missing," Del said, "Thanks, son, for reminding me."

The May family did not talk much and went to bed early.

It was late when Hank came back to the apartment. Bingo did not bother to get up when he heard him coming back. Hank stumbled to the bed and was soon asleep.

Bingo was glad that the man did not kick him again. His side still hurt and he limped when he tried to walk. He was thirsty and hungry. "Why doesn't Delly, or Del, or Betty, or Joe, or Luke, or Charley come after me?" Bingo wondered.

The man got up late the next morning. He did not feed Bingo, but he gave Bingo some water to drink. Hank sit in the old worn out chair and Bingo smelled the terrible odder again. This time he did not lye down again. "I'm going out to get a newspaper, dog, so don't bark," Hank said.

Hank was not gone very long. He came in with a newspaper and laid it on the small table. "I wonder if there are any jobs listed in today's paper?" he asked himself. He opened the paper and Bingo waited. "@$#%$%@, there just isn't any jobs anywhere in this

#$@^$% city," Hank shouted. "We're going to have to go somewhere else to for a #@$#%^$ job," he yelled.

Bingo tried to scoot under the bed.

"@$#%^$% dog, don't act like you are afraid of me!" Hank said and kicked Bingo again. He went back to his chair and the odder was stronger. Bingo laid back by the door. Hank sat in the chair and rocked back and forth. Suddenly he stopped. He looked at the front of the newspaper still on the table. Hank picked up the paper again. "This is my lucky day?" he exclaimed.

"I'd like to keep you boy, but one-thousand dollars is a lot of money," Hank said. "But how can I exchange you for the reward and not be arrested for stealing you?" he asked Bingo.

Hank thought for awhile. "I have an idea," he said and picked up the telephone and called the listed number under Bingo's picture.

Del answered right away.

"Is this the party that has lost a dog?" Hank asked.

"Yes, have you found him," Del asked.

"Is your reward for real?" Hank asked.

"Yes, and it will be in cash," Del answered. "Do you have Franco," he asked.

"No, I don't have your #$%#%%$ dog." Hank shouted, "But I saw him, and I know a way to get him away from the people that have him," he lied. "It will be dangerous to get him." Hank hung up the phone. "I'll let him think about it before I call him back," he said with a laugh.

Del thought the man on the phone was just joking and it was a strange phone call. He prayed for someone to call that knew where Franco really was.

"If the guy is willing to pay one-thousand dollars, he might just pay more," Hank said. He called Del's number again. "I'm the man that called earlier," Hank said. "I've been thinking about how I can steal your dog, but it will be very dangerous for me." "Are you sure your dog is worth only one-thousand dollars?" he asked.

"How much do you want?" Del asked.

"Well, it's going to be dangerous to get him and I wouldn't take the chance for less than two-thousand dollars." Hank answered.

"I'll pay you two-thousand dollars to get Franco back, but how do I know you will have the right dog?" Del asked.

"I have the right @#@$#%^$ dog!" Hank shouted, "You get the two-thousand dollars in small bills, and I'll tell you how we are going to exchange the dog for the money." "Do you know where Pine Woods Park is located?' he asked.

"Yes," Del answered.

"Okay, this is the plan, Hank said, "I'll meet you there at nine o'clock Monday morning. I'll be wearing a ski mask, and a soon as you hand me the money, I'll give you your dog."

"I'll be there with the money," Del replied.

"If you bring anyone with you, you will not get your dog back, understand?" Hank asked.

"I'll be there, alone," Del answered. He heard the phone go dead. He prayed that the man had Franco and not some other dog.

"Be careful, this could be dangerous," Harriett said before she left for work.

"Good luck, Dad," Delly said when he crawled out of the car to go into the school building. "I'm going to believe that when you pick me up this evening, Franco will be in the front seat with you."

Del drove directly to Pine Woods Park from school. This made him thirty minutes early. He drove around the park several times, but he did not see anyone in the park. "Maybe the weather is too cold," Del told himself. He parked the car and walked through the small park. Del heard footsteps behind him. He turned around and faced a tall, skinny, man wearing a black ski mask.

"Where's the money?" the man asked.

"Where's my dog?" Del asked.

"Let me see the money first!" the man shouted.

Del took the money from his pocket.

"Let me see you count the money," the man shouted.

Del help up the money and counted twenty one-hundred dollar bills.

The man tried to grab the money.

Del was angry and jerked the money away. "Where's my dog?" he asked. Del held onto the money tight enough that is would tear if the man tried to pull it out of his hands.

"Over there!" the man shouted.

Del looked behind him. He saw Bingo tied to a tree about twenty yards away.

The man grabbed the money and squeezed it tightly, turned around, and ran behind a row of trees.

Del ran to 'Bingo and released his leash from the tree. "Come on, boy," Del said. He did not take time to pet Bingo.

Bingo was so glad to see Del that he didn't need a leash to lead him. He outran Del to the car and they both jumped in. Del drove away from Pine Tree Park as quickly as he could. When they were several blocks away, Del reached over a patted Bingo on the head. "It's nice to have you back, Franco, even though you look thin and dirty.

"It's nice to be back," Bingo whined in dog language. Bingo was glad to see the traffic, the mountain, and his new home. He did not whine as they passed Joe and Betty's house. He whined with happiness when he saw his new home ahead.

As soon as Del and Bingo were in the house, Del called the newspaper to stop the ad.

"You are very lucky to get your dog back," the newspaper man said.

"Yes, I know," Del replied.

Delly saw Bingo right away. He crawled into the car beside Bingo and gave him a long, long hug. There were tears in the big guy's eyes. "Thank you God, and thanks Dad," Delly said.

"I wish you weren't so friendly with everyone," he told Bingo when they went to bed.

This could be the ending of a great story, but wait, there's more to tell you.

. . .

CHAPTER XIV
Bingo is King

It was almost time for summer vacation. The May family was sitting around the dinner table when Harriett said, "Delly, you are old enough to look for a summer job this year." "What kind of job are you going to look for?" she asked.

"I haven't thought about it," Delly answered. "I guess I just thought we had enough money that I didn't have to work like other kids."

"We have enough, but it's important for you to learn how to work, and how to spend, or save your own money," Del explained. "Let's look through the newspaper this evening and see if there are any summer jobs open."

There were no part-time jobs listed in the paper. The next evening, after school, Del drove Delly to the Job Service office to check on job openings.

"All of our summer jobs are already taken," the lady behind the desk said. "If we get any more we'll let you know, but we have a lot of young people waiting for any jobs that will open up."

"What am I going to do this summer?" Delly asked Del on the way home. He gave Bingo a hug.

"Maybe you can check with our neighbors and see if you can mow their lawns and take care of their flowers," Del answered.

Delly checked with all the neighbors for two blocks. Everyone had already hired help or was doing the yard work themselves.

"Now what am I going to do?" Delly asked that evening.

"Maybe you can think of a business of your own," Harriett replied.

"Like what? I'm too old to run a Lemonade Stand," Delly said.

"You did a good job of building Franco's doghouse," Del said. "Maybe you could build dog houses and sell them for a summer job,"

"It took me two weeks to build the dog house," Delly replied, "It cost one-hundred dollars to build it. I would have to ask a price of two-hundred to make any money for the time I spend. I don't think anyone would pay me two-hundred dollars for a dog house when they can buy one at Wal-Mart for less than a hundred."

"I'm sure you will think of something," Harriett said.

After dinner Delly went outside to play with Bingo. He stuck his head in the door a little later and yelled, "Franco and I are going to walk down the hill behind the house. We will be back in an hour," he said,

"Be sure you are home before dark," Del replied.

Delly and Bingo walked through the back gate of the new fence. They walked into an area that did not have any houses. They stopped to rest on the back side of the hill. "Those mountains are pretty but soon more houses will be built and it will be hard to see the mountains from here," Delly told Bingo.

"But, the mountains will never be as pretty as you, Franco. You are so pretty that too many people have wanted you," Delly said. "It's too bad that there is only one of you."

Delly jumped to his feet. "That's it!" he shouted. "I know what my new business will be if you will help me." Delly ran toward the house with Bingo running beside him.

Bingo did not understand what Delly had said, but Delly was happy so he was happy.

"Mom, Dad, I know what business I can start!" Delly exclaimed.

Harriett sat down in her chair beside Del. "All right. Let's hear about this new business," she said.

Delly was so excited that he could hardly talk. "Well, it's a cool business that can be going the year around, not just for the summer," Delly said.

"That sounds nice," Del replied.

"Well, Franco is a pretty dog, right?" Delly asked.

"Yes, we know that," his parents said.

"And a lot of people have wanted him, right?" Delly asked.

"It seems that way," Del answered. I can name at least five."

"What if we had a lot of little Francos to sell?" Delly asked.

"Where are you going to get little Franco's to sell?" Del asked.

"Find Franco a mate and let him raise a family!" Delly shouted.

Harriett fell back into her chair. "My heavens!" she exclaimed. "I only agreed to one dog, not any more!"

"But, Mom, they wouldn't be in the house," Delly explained. "I can build some shelters in the back yard so they can stay outside. I'll take care of them, Mom, and it won't be any more work for you, I promise."

"The city would not let us raise and sell dogs in this part of the city," Harriett said, "They won't even let people park their vehicles outside their garages for very long."

"We can go ask the mayor about it tomorrow," Delly said. "Can we Dad?" he asked.

"It has to be all right with your mother first, son," Del answered.

"Can we Mom, please!" Delly begged.

"I must be crazy and should have my head examined but go ahead and see what the mayor says," Harriett said, "I'm sure he will say no."

"Even if the mayor says yes, Delly, where can you find a female dog as pretty as Franco?" Del asked. "You have to be careful that the pups are as pretty as Franco."

"We can probably find one at one of the pet stores in town," Delly answered.

"You'll have to figure the expense of buying a female, and a lot of dog food," Del reminded Delly.

"I can't believe this is happening!" Harriett exclaimed.

The next morning Del and Delly drove down town to the mayor's office.

"The mayor is very busy," the secretary said. "Do you have an appointment?" she asked.

"No," Del answered. "Would you mind if we just sit here and wait to see if he can make time to see us?" he asked.

"I'll tell him you are here," the secretary said. She pushed a button on her desk. "There are a couple of people here to see you, Mr. Mayor," she said.

"I'm busy with someone right now," the mayor said over the intercom. "I'm not sure I can see them this morning."

"We will wait," Del said. He and Delly sit down in some comfortable chairs in the nice office. They were looking through the large windows facing the mountains. "I never get tired of looking at those mountains," Del said.

"Me either," Delly agreed.

Just then the mayor's door opened and two men came out. The mayor came out behind them. "We will meet again when we get all the information on that project that we need," the mayor said. He was walking over to the secretary's desk when he saw Del and Delly. "Why didn't you tell me my neighbors were here to see me?" he asked the secretary with a smile. "Come on in," he said.

The mayor pointed to two chairs in his office. "Is this a social call or do you have some business to discuss with me?" he asked.

"This is business," Del answered.

"I'm sorry we don't have an appointment. Delly has an idea for a business but he needs to ask your approval first." "Tell Mr. Mayor you idea, Delly," Del said.

"Well, I can't find a summer job," Delly said.

"Yes, I know," the mayor said, "We had a few jobs open up in this building, but they were filled the day we let people know about them." "What is your plan, Delly?" he asked.

"Well, we have a beautiful dog," Delly begin.

"Yes I know. I've seen him a few times, the mayor said.

"Franco is a special dog; so special that he has been stolen several times," Delly explained.

"I think I saw your ad and reward in the paper," the mayor replied. "I thought it looked like your dog anyway."

"Well, we have decided that since Franco is so popular, we might be able to raise and sell his pups," Delly said. "But we didn't know if it would be allowed in our part of the city."

"I'm glad you came to talk to me first, Delly," the mayor said. "This shows that you are going to be a good businessman. The city laws say that you could have a litter of pups since you have a fenced back yard, and if the animals are not too noisy, and you keep the place clean." "But, you are not allowed to sell anything in our part of the city. You'll have to sell them somewhere else." He explained.

"That's all right," Delly replied. "I don't think we would have any trouble selling them to the pet stores downtown."

"Sounds good to me," the mayor replied. He stood up and shook Delly's hand. "Welcome to the world of business, young man,"

"Thanks," Delly said. He felt really cool and grown up.

"Thanks for taking time for us, Neighbor," Del said. "We know you are very busy."

"My meeting was over a little early and good luck Mr. Delly Mays," he said.

"Now we have to find Franco a mate," Delly said.

Del drove to the nearest pet shop. He and Delly left Bingo in the car with the doors locked. They looked at all the dogs. There were no dogs that were as large, or pretty as Bingo. "Here is our phone number in case you get one," Delly said.

"I think I know what you are looking for, so I'll call you if I find a female like that," the shop owner said.

Del and Delly looked in every pet shop in the city. There were no large, pretty, female dogs anywhere. "This is going to be harder than I thought," Delly said.

Del needed to get back home to rest. Delly fixed two glasses of iced tea and gave Bingo fresh water and a doggie treat. Bingo lay next to Del's chair. "I think I'll check the newspaper to see if any dogs are listed," Delly said. He turned to the back section where animals for sale were listed.

"Dad, this might be something," Delly said. "Dogs to give away: part Husky and German Shepherd, friendly, three males and one female, 1426 Old Gold Camp Road," he read. "Can we go look at them?" Delly asked.

"I wish I had as much energy as you and Franco have," Del said getting out of his chair.

"Come on Franco. We're going to try to find you a wife!" Delly exclaimed.

Del drove out of the city, and then he stopped the car. "Would you like to drive the rest of the way?" he asked Delly.

"Sure, Dad," Delly said. The two men changed places. Bingo stayed in the middle.

At Gold Camp Road they checked the house numbers to be sure they were going in the right direction. They passed ten places and most of them had horses and dogs. "Here it is," Delly said as he turned into a small driveway. The house was almost hidden behind evergreen trees. Three large, friendly dogs greeted them. They were pretty dogs, but they were all males.

"I hope they haven't already given the female away," said Delly.

The dogs were barking. The door of the house opened and a man came out. Delly saw another large, pretty dog following the man. It was a female.

"We are looking for a female dog," Delly explained. "Is this the one you want to give away?" he asked.

"I thought we would, but we have decided to keep her and just give away the males," the man said. "Which male would you like to have?" he asked.

Delly felt disappointed. The female was almost as large and pretty as Bingo. "We have to have a female," Delly explained. "We are looking for a mate for the dog that we have in the car."

The man walked over to the car and looked at Bingo through the window. Bingo sit tall and proud. "Oh," the man said. He noticed the nice vehicle and the nice clothes Del and Delly were wearing. "We really love the dog, and we want her to have a good home," the man said, "We wanted to keep all the dogs, but they grew too large to take care of and they eat an awful lot of dog food."

"Can we have the female dog, please?" Delly asked.

The man stood quietly for a minute. "We really like the dog . . ." he said again.

"I'll give you fifty dollars for her," Delly said.

"That will buy a lot of dog food for the others," the man said. "It's a deal."

Del gave the man five ten-dollar bills. "Thanks," the man said.

Delly went to the car and got one of Bingo's collars and leashes. He put them on the female dog and led her to the car. Bingo saw the dog and jumped into the back seat. He tried to crawl under the seat. All he could do was hide his nose. Bingo put his paws over his eyes.

The three men laughed.

"Good luck," the man said before he went back into the house. The other three dogs followed him.

Delly put the female in the front seat. "I won't embarrass Franco any more right now," he said.

Del drove back to the city. "You sounded like a real business man today, son," he said.

"Thanks, Dad," Delly replied. He patted the new dog on the head whenever she seemed nervous.

"What are you going to name her?" Del asked.

Delly thought for a long time. "I think I'll call her Tammy O because that rhymes with Franco," he answered.

Tammy O jumped out of the car just like the Mays place had always been her home. Delly showed Tammy O the back yard, unleashed her chain so she could run and play behind the tall fence, and then he went back to the car after Bingo.

Bingo was still lying on the floor with his head down. "Come on, Franco, you'll like her," Delly said. He pulled Bingo out of the car and to the back yard. Delly pushed Bingo through the gate and took of his leash. "Now you two get acquainted," he said and shut the gate.

Bingo ran behind the garage.

Tammy O ran after him.

Bingo ran up the steps to his throne on the high deck.

Tammy was right behind him.

Bingo backed up against the railing of the deck and Tammy O came right up to him. He could not move. Bingo looked at the new dog. She was pretty. She was as pretty as the black and white collie. "She seems to like me," Bingo thought. "Will she run away like the black and white collie did?" He remembered that scary night that he had seen the big, big cat.

Tammy O whined.

Bingo knew she was trying to be brave and friendly in a new place. She needed a friend. Bingo ran down the steps and Tammy O chased him. Bingo chased Tammy O. They were soon having a good time together.

Bingo and
Annie-O
are in
Love ♡

Delly was anxious to show his mother his new business. He took Harriett to the back yard as soon as she came in from work.

Harriett watched the two dogs playing. "It's a miracle that you found a dog as pretty as Franco," she said. "If the pups are as pretty as their parents, you should have no trouble selling them. Remember that taking care of them, and keeping the yard clean, is your responsibility."

"Mom says you can sleep in the house tonight," Delly said.

Tammy O was so well behaved that she was soon sleeping in the house next to Bingo. Del bought a van that was large enough to take both dogs when they went somewhere. Tammy O was soon as spoiled as Bingo.

Bingo and Tammy O took many walks with Delly that summer. Summer was soon over and Delly started his second year of high school. In The Fall, Tammy O started to get fat but she could still run with Delly and Bingo across the hills.

"Delly we need to talk about your business," Harriett said one evening. Delly sat down across the table from Harriett. "I noticed that you haven't built any shelters for the dogs yet and Tammy O is going to have puppies in a few weeks," she said. "I don't want the pups born in the house on my white carpets. You are going to have to train Tammy O to stay in the garage at night, and when we aren't at home."

"I hate to do that, Mom, but you have been great to let her stay in the house this long," Delly replied.

"I'll see if I can find a heater for the garage since it is getting so cold outside."

"I have one in the store that you can use," Harriett said. "That will help you keep down your expenses for awhile."

It was hard for Bingo to decide whether to sleep in Delly's room or in the garage with Tammy O. He tried to sleep in the house the first night but he was restless. Delly finally put him in the garage in the middle of the night.

The first snow was falling outside. Tammy O had cried all night. Bingo did not know what to do to help her. He just stayed in the garage all day beside Tammy O.

Del went to school to pick up Delly that evening. "Delly, Tammy O hasn't had her puppies yet and I think we might need to call the vet," Del said.

Delly went to the garage to be with Tammy O while Del called the vet. "I'll come out and examine her in about an hour," Dr. Oakley said. "I'm here alone and can't leave until my helper comes back."

The doctor was a little early and examined Tammy O. "The pups should have been born by now," he said. "I need to take her to the clinic so I can operate on her if I need to," he said.

Delly helped the doctor lift Tammy O and put her in the back of the vet's animal hospital wagon. Tammy O cried as they carefully laid her down.

"She is not going to die, is she Dr. Oakley?" Delly asked.

"I sure hope not, son," Dr. Oakley answered. "I'll do my best to save her."

The Mays followed the hospital wagon to the doctor's clinic. They sit in the waiting room and waited. The Mays family wanted to cry every time they heard Tammy O cry. Bingo tried to lye beside Delly's chair but he was restless.

"Poor Franco, he doesn't know what is going on," Harriett said patting Bingo on the head.

The doctor finally came in to the room. "We had to do surgery, but Tammy O is all right and so are the ten puppies," he said.

"Ten puppies!" Harriett, Del, and Delly all exclaimed at once. "Thank you Lord!"

"Maybe ten puppies will make enough money to pay for the doctor bills," Delly said hopefully.

Tammy O and the ten puppies were able to go home the next day. Tammy O's stitches were removed a week later. She seemed to have enough milk for all her babies but some always had to wait in line. Although she would run with Bingo, she never went far from her puppies. After two weeks the puppies eyes opened and they begin to wiggle all over the garage. Bingo was soon used to the pups crawling all over him and pulling on his ears.

Delly hated to go to school for a few days. It would have been more fun to stay home with his new business. With his studies and football, he did not have much time to spend with his new family. Del watched the puppies and made sure that all of them were able to nurse every time. He enjoyed helping with Delly's new business.

It is a warm wintry day. Bingo sits up on the deck of the house. He looks at the city below. He looks at the beautiful mountains, and then he looks at his beautiful family. Betty is visiting and playing with the puppies. Bingo sits proudly, and he feels like a king. Maybe he is a king. Weeks go by.

"Delly, the pups are six weeks old now," Del said. "It's time for you to cal the pet shops and sell them."

"Oh Dad, do I have to?" Delly asked.

"There are hard days in any business, Delly," Del said with a smile. "You can find out which store will give you the best price and take them one of the pups for people to see. We can keep the others until they sell.

I guess that was the deal," Delly replied. "But I don't know which one to take to the store, they are all so cute. Should I take Sparky, Jumpy, or Happy, or Daisy, or Tammo, or Banbo, or Franco Jr., or Blacko, or Wolfco, or Little Franco?"

"I think you know which one to take," Del said.

"Yeah, I'll take Little Franco because he the largest and prettiest one," Delly replied.

The one store down town offered five hundred dollars for the pup. Delly is going to make five thousand dollars his first year. He paid his parents three hundred dollars for dog food, five hundred dollars for Tammy O's hospital bill, and put the rest in his savings.

The second year Tammy O had eight puppies and did not need surgery.

Many homes have become happy places with little Bingos. The May's place has the sounds of happy dogs. And, King Bingo sits on his throne and enjoys one day at a time. God loves you more than He loves Bingo and He wants you happy too.

THE END